INFORMATION INDUSTRY FUTURE DEVELOPMENT

JOHN LOK

ISBN 979-888555832-7

Contents

Preface

Introduction

Nowadays, we are encountering information technological development period. Does information technological development bring economic growth? Why and how can information technological development influence our daily lives change? Has information technological development and economy close relationship? This book divides two parts. Part one explains how information technological development, such as internet invention to be applied to ecommerce, smart phone and mobile game products how to bring macro GDP income to global. Part two explains how to research other scientific technology to compare information technology to evalute whether these both information technology and scientific technology which can bring long term GDP income to global industries.All of these questions in this book, I shall indicate examples to explain whether they have cause and effect close relationship as well as how information technology change our future lives in possible.

Readers can learn more human economic development knowledge how it can be influenced by information technological development, such as internet ecommerce, smart phones, mobile game information technological products as well as other scientific technological products to bring technology development how influences our daily living as well as brings global economic growth. I shall also explain that why and how information technology can influence internet ecommerce and smart mobile and mobile games procucts as well as other scientifical technological product, such as artificial intelligence, will be important to raise GDP income source to future any developed and development countries both.

Prologue

Table of content

CHAPTER ONE

Living information economy environment raises our environment protection awareness

In the future, when our economic environment causes to change suddenly variable significantly, it can also influence our living environment changes, then it will also influences our living behaviors change in order to choose to earn the most large benefits in effect. I shall our daily some living cases to explain why it has relationship between our living environment and our living economy and our living behaviors.

The first living changing case, I shall indicate how living economic environment influences students' learning behaviors and social employable behaviors change both.

When one country's students have much pressure to learn and there are many students need to enter schools to learn, but the country has less schools to supply to them to learn. Then, this living economic environment changing factor, e.g. there are many parents need to go to work, but they have no enough money to support their adult age students, e.g. 20 years university students to let them have enough money to continue to enroll universities to learn. IN this less university supplying number and many poor families living economic environment both factors, it will cause many students feel pressure to enroll any one university, if every year, there has about 100,000 number secondary school students at least, they prepare to pass examination to enroll any one university to study in the country. But, every university has only 100 to 200 secondary students who have enroll to any one university successfully. However, the country has only two universities are existence. So, it has possible that there are 98,600 to 98,800 secondary students , they can not enroll to any one university to study in the country every year. These secondary only choose to find jobs to do.

But, their educational level is low, they will feel find jobs to do in difficulty. If the country's jobs supplying number is less. For example, in the year, there are only 80,000 secondary level jobs to be supplied to these secondary level students to do. Hence, in the year, this country will have 18,600 to 18,800 secondary students who can not find any jobs to work , even they will lose jobs (unemployment) in the whole year in possible.

So in living economic view, this low jobs supplying environment and the low university number graduation and many secondary schools students unemployment factor will only cause this society's economic environment to be more poor, because when it have many secondary students who can not find any jobs to do easily, then they do easy to do stealing, fighting etc. crime behaviors to influence the society's living safety to it living people every day. It is due to this country lacks enough universities to provide to these secondary students to learn as well as they must feel more pressure to examination , due to the university enrolling demand must be raised, e.g. five A grades at minimum. They need to earn in order to enroll to any one university to learn. Even, although some secondary students, they can enroll to any one university to study, but many their parents are poor families and they can not continue to them to enroll any one private university to study, I suppose this country has none any government universities existence. So, these private universities are only for the rich families whose children can enroll to learn successfully. I will let many poor students who feel unfair because they have the best examination result to enroll to any one of these two university to study, but because their parents have no enough money to support them to enroll to either one of these two universities to study. So, they will also need to attempt to find low education level jobs to do in society. Hence, it will raise secondary students competitive number, it will bring negative influence in society, e.g. unemployment rate will be difficult to go down and it will climb up in possible, if this country's low education level jobs supplying number can not increase significantly in the whole year. Then, in this poor living environment economic factor will impact social crime rate increases and young's committing suicide behaves will also increases. If this country can not find methods to solve universities supplying number and secondary student education level jobs supply number shortages, secondary students feel learning pressure emotion psychological problem, poor families living and low salary level household earner psychological pressure problem for this poor and low education level age stakeholder in society. Hence, solving the young age stakeholder learning and working problem will be this country's major social problem if it still hopes its economic environment can be improved.

It must need to change their living and learning condition to be better, it can not neglect to take care their psychological need. It can not only depend on take care the rich families stakeholder's living needs, e.g. supplying enough cars to be imported to let them buy or building expensive houses to let them buy. It is one wrong direction to change this country's economic development, e.g. GDP increases aim. This country ought not need only considerate how to import more cars and build house to achieve the business income increasing aim. It ensures to be one wrong direction to raise economic growth in society. Because it's living standard of many poor families must not be improved absolutely. It ought arrange resources

to help education investors to invest more money to build universities in order to increase universities number between five to seven more in order to solve the education challenge to let many secondary students can enroll to universities to study. These universities can have three government assistance governments in order to many secondary school students can pay cheap tuition fee and government can support education loan to them to continue to finish their degrees as well as government can provide business loans to assist some businessmen to start up their businesses in order to increase job positions to let many secondary level education level students have jobs to do. I suppose that this country has enough high education level jobs to supply to university graduates to do. Finally, it also needs to support unemployment assistance allowance to some unemployed parents in short time. It aims to encourage them to continue to seek job. When they have jobs to do, they can not get this employment assistance allowance from government.

So, they will need to continue to contribute their effort to serve their society. For example, government only provide the unemployment assistance allowance to these building workers and helping them to seek the new construction employers in short time when they unemployed, e.g. within one month. They will need continue to go to interview when government had arranged the construction firm to make appointment to meet them. If they are failure to pass the interview, then government will continue to help them to find another construction firm as well as arranging the another interview time. So, if they can achieve any one time interview, the government will not

provide another interview chance and it also will not provide the unemployment assistance allowance to them. It aims to encourage unemployed workers continue seek any jobs, it does not encourage them to earn any government assistance allowance in long time.

ON conclusion, it is one best method to change any countries' living environment to the low education and low salary people when the country's government can arrange to use the resources from rich people to be used for the poor people's living and job and learning needs, such as building more government schools, providing short time unemployment assistance allowance, building many public and low market price of houses for the poor and low education young age stakeholders in themselves societies nowadays.

● How investment invention and scientific discovery influences our future living economic development

ON the second living economic environment influence aspect, I shall indicate our invention and scientific discovery will be one important factor influences our future living model has much changed to be improved better. I shall explain how it brings our living economic environment changes as below:

Orthodox growth theories regard scientific discovery of invention as the ultimate determinants of the

rate of growth of productivity. Investment is merely required to match the pace of scientific advance or invention. However, Schmookler has provided evidence for the conclusion that the rate of invention is determined by the rate of investment. IN fact, inventions are best regarded as a form of investment, and their volume depends, in like manner, on their expected profitability. Investment opportunities are recreated by un limit attempting investment. There is no evidence that inventive opportunities in a particular field become exhausted for technical reasons, although they may do so for economic reasons.

Invention may not be succession, but there is a high probabilities that prior circumstances will bring them about , as the existence of near-simultaneous discoveries by different people show. Learning from prior experience is important not just in scientific or engineering matters, but in other fields such as business and social organization. So, the improvement of scientific advance can thus be neglected in constructing a theory of economy growth, at least at the beginning. Research and development can be achieved with other forms of investment and not considered separately at this stage.

So, it brings this question: How can the relation between investment, invention and scientific discovery bring economic growth to improve our living standard in possible? We need to discuss this question is by how we plan to implement the exploitation of scientific discoveries. According to this view, scientific advance that ultimately determines the rate of growth of productivity. Investment is required to match the kind of scientific invention. If it is more than sufficient for that purpose, the rate of scientific invention return will fall, and if it is less, the rate of return will rise. The productivity possibility frontier, or the production function, shifts outward at a rate determined ultimately by the kind of scientific invention. At alternative view, it is the kind of invention that is the determining factor, with the kind of scientific invention more in the background. But is either view, we need to know about the relations between investment, invention and scientific discovery.

Furthermore, there is no evidence that any investment chance must be success to achieve any new scientific invention or discoveries. but since human decides to continue without limited learning opportunities. Consequently, instead of scientific discovery and invention being the creators of investment opportunities, investment itself creates them. To understand economic growth, therefore, we need to examine the rate, quality, and determinants of investment. It is a mistake to treat scientific invention and invention as processes that are independent of investment. Any new scientific invention or discovery which are needed human' talent and attributing time and nervous. So, training new scientists and increasing new scientists number will be needed because we need they solve our social problems, e.g. air and ocean water environment pollution, overpopulation causes food shortage and water shortage, land shortage dues to global warming causes global water level is increasing. Any non discovery scientific products invention, instead of artificial intelligent products, it is possible that scientists can invent any new technological products to replace them to provide to human to use for our living innovative needs.

As Schmookler does not deny that in some " science -based" industries (he mentions the electrical, electronic, nuclear, chemical , and drug and pharmaceutical industries) invention and research is heavily dependent on scientific knowledge, and that in these industries there were many instances of important inventions being directly induced by scientific discoveries. However, he argues that, even in these industries , economically evaluated technical problems and opportunities arising in the normal conduct of business are dominant' (p.68).

Hence, scientific discovery is also one important factor to bring any invention in success. Also, it implies that scientific knowledge is needed, but if out society can have many scientists are created by education. Then, any new kinds of scientific discoveries will have much chances to find in success. So, increasing the number of scientists will bring the more chance to achieve any new scientific discoveries, scientific knowledge is the traditional and basic education concept. In our future, scientific discoveries is more important to compare general scientific knowledge if we hope we societies can be improved to live more comfortable as well as our living standard will also been raising by more new scientific discoveries.

The third living economic environment aspect is human development. The current economic crisis has affected all aspects of life resulting in political instability, personal financial troubles and a growing number of business bankruptcies. How to use effective human development policy to prevent the economic crisis threats. I shall indicate that governments ought to consider how to apply human development strategy to prevent the economic recession crisis occurrence to threaten to influence whose social economic growth in these aspects.

On high quality education and health systems aspect. Different country's government ought to concern, due to it can support the productivity of an economy by providing healthy and highly trained individuals. Because of the country has good human development strategy, then it can use talent labors to assist its economic growth and good governance practices by governments easily. It seems that human development, good governance and economic growth has close relationship, so it can reduce the economic recession during times of crisis occurrence. It means that human development can influence economic growth. Economic development implies both the improvement of people's health education and general well being and the presence of positive economic indicates, such as economic growth and low unemployment with economic development, people will have better education and healthcare and be more productive. Better human development nations tend to have lower crime rates and greater political strategy than less human development nations.

Does it bring positive consequence of human development to prevent economic recession? It will be an important resource to influence economic growth. How does this human development public policy solve economic crisis? Whether can government use of fiscal policy, such as human development to assist economic stabilization to promote growth and the increase of the capital income efficiency? A key issue relates to the effect of how to use public expenditure and its financing to spend human development on effects of fiscal policy by using a time series approach.

A general model that includes expenditure on education and health, which influences human capital, expenditure and health administration, public investment and transfers and consumption of public products four kinds of expenditure. The model can be used to explore and impact of human development expenditure used on long run per capita income. Debt and external and financing are also possible to be spent to human development expenditure in the general model. So, the public expenditure on the long run per capita income can be explored for low, lower, middle and upper-middle income countries policy that is needed to be estimated how to spend for each aspect of human development expenditure to assist to every country's economy development.

A time series perspective is explained on economic growth may be more useful to pursue for growth and human development strategies. A time series can allow to pursue time series studies for particular countries or country groups at particular stages of economic growth. It can allow for a more specific micro behavior of economic agents. In general, any country has three income groups, such as low income, lower-middle income and upper middle income groups. Also, any country may have these four types of public expenditure for human development which including: enhancing education and building up of human capital, public investment to finance general market and subsistence production, e.g. transportation system, such as roads, bridges, harbors, water supply, sanitation, health and care and education.

A 2005 year study had been carried by Dimonson, Marsh & Staunton, which performed an analysis is stock returns in 53 countries, going back to 1900 year for 17 countries, did not find evidence of a significant long term positive relationship between GDP growth rates and equity returns. Also the analysis from Schroders Economics team found that over the past sixty years, there has tended to be a positive relationship between GDP growth and equity market returns during the recovery, expansion and slowdown phases of the traditional business cycle. This relationship has traditionally broken down during the recession phase.

The Schroders economics team also indicated a traditional business cycle model, which has four stages. In the beginning, it is slowdown stage. It means output above trend, growth decelerating and inflation rising. Next is recession stage. It means output below trend, growth developing, inflation falling. Then, it is recovery stage. It means output below trend, growth decelerating, inflation falling. Finally, it is expansion stage, it means output above trend growth accelerating, inflation is rising. The economic team also suggested the traditional business cycle model: In the slowdown stage, GDP growth is positive, but falling, inflation is high and rising, so policy strategy is tight recommended in the recession stage, GDP growth is negative and falling, inflation is falling. So, policy strategy is loosening recommended. In the recovery stage, GDP growth is negative and rising, inflation is low and falling, so policy strategy is loose recommended. Finally, the expansion stage, GDP growth is positive and rising, inflation is rising, so policy strategy is tightening recommended.

It seems that governments ought concern the business cycle period to evaluate themselves country GDP growth to achieve the most effective policy to adopt to achieve different human development policies to invest to present economic recession crisis occurrence. Usually, in the recovery and expansion phases of the business cycle, the stock market tends to perform well as rising GDP and earnings growth drives positive excess returns on equity. In the slowdown phase, inflation is still high and monetary policy remains tight, resulting in s difficult environment for corporations. reducing earnings and stock valuations tends to result in negative excess returns for equities: declining GDP growth is therefore usually matched with poor equity performance. It also explained that during the recession phase, there is often GDP growth is falling, but the excess return on equity tends to be positive. Historically, falling inflation and an accompanying loosening of monetary policy is needed to rise re-rating.

Thus, it seems the business cycle and human development policy has close relationship. During in the slowdown stage, GDP growth is positive, but falling, inflation is high and rising, then the country's government ought spend less expenditures to human development because GDP growth is stable growth. Otherwise, during it is recession stage or recovery stage, it means output below trend, growth developing, inflation falling. Then the country's government ought spend more to invest to any human development needs to prepare to raise whose labor productivity and GDP growth. Finally, during the expansion stage, GDP growth is positive and rising, inflation is rising. Then the country's government can spend less expenditures to invest human development. Thus, any country's government ought concern what is whose country's business cycle stage to arrange to spend more or less expenditures to achieve its human development policy in different business cycle stages.

Nowadays, political scientists began to apply quantitative methods to classify and measure political interactions. In general, any countries' policies that maximize growth are optimal that cares solely about pure " capitalists". The greater, the inequality of wealth and income, the higher rate of taxation and the lower growth. It shows that inequality in land and income ownership is negatively with subsequent economic growth. Many economists have tried to explain lower growth rates and unemployment with a growing tax burden in many developed countries. Although, the impact of taxes on growth can be observed both from the aspect of efficiency and aspect of changes in equity that taxes introduce to economy.

I shall indicate how to apply quantitative evidence to review policy to review human development strategy. In fact, economic or welfare outcomes to changes in regulatory policy has close relationship to be suggested outcome indicate to reduce risk face economic recession occurrence to any countries. Every country government ought design to gather quantitative data to prepare any policy implementation to support mutual learning and best practice in different societal and market conditions. The goal is to help countries to build better government systems and implement policies at both national and regional level that lead to sustainable economic and social development.

The critical public policy challenge is to ensure that the expected economic benefits from regulatory changes are both achieved and outweigh any economic cost imposed. I shall indicate evidence on the outcomes of regulatory policies to help policymakers how design regulatory measures that work better. This method is called "regulatory management". This regulatory management study suggests some conclusions to any policymakers as below:

● Firstly, poorly designed policy regulation can not raise economic activities and ultimately reduce economic growth.
● Secondly, it is impossible between a regulatory policy change and the impact on economic outcomes, such as economic growth is from statistic method easily.
● Thirdly, the reliance on economic recession analysis to investigate the relationship across countries between regulatory variables and economic outcomes may not be readily applicable to any countries and may not always be expressed in economic values. It is particularly useful in developing countries regulatory policy measures for recommendation to policymakers only.
● Fourthly, most quantitative studies deal with the costs of regulation and give little or no attention to quantifying the benefits of regulation. For the policymaker, it is important to compare the estimated costs of regulation. Any policy regulation is intended to correct market failures and assist to economic efficiency and growth. The public policy aims to reduce socially unacceptable income and wealth distributions or it can satisfy expectation that the public should have access to certain products and services, e.g. health care and education irrespective of ability to pay, such as merit products. Some of regulation, that governments need to concern, e.g. of property rights, company law, law of contract etc. and regulation can provide important economic and social, including environmental benefits.

Of course, those benefits need to be set against the costs. Because regulations are the operations of effective economies and societies to market rules, e.g. law of contract and protecting property rights and the rights of citizens. It seems regulatory management is important to influence any policies can be achieved effectively, due to one good regulation can supervise the leader's behavior and otherwise one bad regulation can not supervise the leader's behavior, even it can not assist the country economic growth for long term. So, any leader needs to concern how to use quantitative evidence to review human development policy if who hopes whose policy's regulations are achieved effectively.

At the same time, economic, environmental and welfare pressures raise the demand for regulation above minimum needed for operating a market economy to prepare to face the economic recession occurrence. So, evidence on the outcomes of regulatory policies should help policymakers design regulatory measures that work better. Similarly, evidence on the success or failure of regulation can be used for public accountability purposes.

Regulatory policy defines as the process by which government, when identifying a policy objectives, decides whether to use regulation as a policy instrument and proceeds to draft and adopt a regulation through evidence based decision making. The strategy shall commit governments to remain a regulatory management system, articulating regulatory policy goals, and the impacts of regulation on competitiveness and economic growth. For example, regulation, such as employment law or competition law, the regulation of employment law is applied to control any employers' behaviors to give the fair treatment to whose employees and to protect employees' benefits.

Besides the regulation of competition law is applied to control the fair competition in market. Why this regulations has direct relationship to economy growth. An identifiable economy theory of specific regulatory policies, e.g. administrative simplification and specific economic and welfare outcomes, e.g. high economic growth. The result is a series about the impact of regulatory management on economic indicators. There can be set out as a causal. Thus regulation can be supportive of market transactions and may result in significant economic, social and environmental benefits.

At the same time, ill-designed regulation can have appreciable economic costs, leading to the concept of regulatory burden. In particular, good regulation can reduce the chance of lower economic growth or GDP occurrence, damage investment and competitiveness. But, it has also weakness, such as regulatory costs may act as a barrier to entry into industry in the form of set up cost, e.g. installing equipment to meet health and safety laws and on going annual cost, e.g. preparing returns and facilities inspections.

However, regulatory can be unduly costly to comply with administrator and enforce, but it simplification can reduce the regulatory burden. For example, regulation may not only affect the behavior of those targeted by a rule (direct effects), but invoke behavioral change in the economy (indirect effects). Whether regulation can support governments to avoid or reduce the threats of economic recession occurrence, it depends on the leader's concern how to use quantitative evidence to review policy before who decides to implement which kinds of regulatory management methods.

In recent year, some countries had considered how to achieve policy field with a view to introducing better regulation. The aim is to ensure that regulation occurs only when it does improve social welfare and that regulatory changes do, so with the minimum net cost or maximum net benefit to society. For a policy making perspective, it is important to appreciate how and why a regulatory achievement can be expected to result in a particular impact.

Causal chain analysis is a technique for explaining the way in which a caused regulatory results in an economic impact. By helping to understand the how and why questions, regulatory impact, so causal chain analysis can provide policymakers, with relevant information on the consequences of their policy decisions. It seems that regulation can lead economic improvements, such as higher GDP growth, higher productivity, move business start ups. etc. Due to the causal chain analysis relates to each component separately. So, any decision maker hopes to achieve better regulation, who needs time to attempt to different regulations to achieve whose policies every year. Then, who can review why whose policy can not improve whose country's economic growth as well as to attempt to find reasons how to apply better regulatory to achieve better policy to improve its country's economic growth. It seems review regulatory policy which ought to concern to any decision maker, if who wanted to achieve better regulatory policy to raise economic and welfare gains every year.

In capitalism view, capitalism tends equal systematically, through not uniformly to reward business behaviour that is honest, fair civil and compassionate. When does irrational honesty behaviour influence social economy development? It concerns behavioral economy to individual decision maker whose individual psychology, social psychology into economics. It helps policy makers to incentive in market transactions and in response to policy interventions. So, policy advisers are already using the finding of behavioural economy to advantage to public policy, there is nothing about behavioural economy, but for a long time, it has tended to be concerned how the social economic development, particularly in macro economy. For example, policy makers concern of money in nominal rather than real terms in whose how to solve to unemployment. Also, policy makers neglect to recognize how economic motivations apart from those based on rational calculation usually. Most, probably of policy decision makers' decisions to will be drawn out over many days to come, who feels action rather than inaction to any decision immediately, and not as the outcome of a weighted average of probabilities. It seems that the policy decision maker's irrational honesty behaviour will influence how our social's economic development to be good or bad.

However, nation leader's behaviour can influence the country's economy development. Concerning irrational honesty whether this behavior can influence social economic development. I shall indicate those questions to attempt to be considered, such as: Can there be a growing scarce without a growing shortage or a growing shortage with a growing scarcity? Can a decision be economic if there is no money in involved? Can there be surplus food in a society where people are hungry? For example, building ordinary and building luxury housing both involves using many of the same resources, such as bricks, pipes, and construction labour. How does the allocation of these resources between ordinary housing and luxury housing tend to change after rent control laws are passed?

When a government institution or program produces counter productive results, is that necessarily a sign of irrationality on the part of those who run that particular institution or program? Why do American manufacturers of computers or television sets tend to have them transported by others? When Chinese manufacturers tend to transport themselves? How did the movement of population from rural to urban America affect the economy of retail selling in the early twentieth century? Advertising even when it is successful, is often considered to be a benefit only to those who advertise, but of no benefit to consumers, who have to pay the cost of the advertisement in the higher price of the products who buy. Is it irrational economy behaviour to society? Why would luxury hotels be charging lower rates than economy hotels? Whether governments choose to protect competition or protect competitors which method is better? What have been some of the economic and social consequences of the substitution of machine power for human strength, as a result of industralization and the growing importance of knowledge, skills and experience in a high-technological economy? How can per capita income be increasing by 50 % over a period of years, when average family income and average householder income remain almost stable over those same year? Does inequality of income tend to be greater or less in long run than in the short run?

All above questions concern the social and economic influences won't be better if the policy decision makers or businessmen do any irrational honesty behaviours. It seems rational honesty behaviour is important to any policy decision makers or businessmen because whose rational or irrational behaviour can influence social economic development directly are driven to act by economic as well as social ethical and other reasons. So economists need to study of what motivates individual acts, especially regarding economic decisions, offers an intellectual challenge to the human sciences. So, if economists can predict to judge whether any policy decision makers or businessmen whose act is irrational or rational, then who can assist the country's economic development more easily.

Promoting honesty in negotiation can influence social economy growth in global. In a competitive and moral imperfect world, business people are often facing with serious ethical challenges. Usually, many businessmen feel justified in engaging in less than ideal conduct to protect their own interests. However, our commonplace that work to promote credibility, trust and honesty of behaviours can influence our social economy growth in long term. For example, deception in negotiation behaviour is immoral, due to success in business typically requires successful negotiations.

Given the high value placed on honesty, the incentives for deception in negotiation create a serious moral tension for business people. Not surprisingly, deception in negotiation is a widely discussed problem in business ethics. How many negotiators their views are essentially, who is regarded as a superior moral philosopher, would find them objectionable? For example, philosophical debates about the loss of civilian life in war would be better served by putting resources and intellectual energy into developing political, economic diplomatic and military strategies that resources and intellectual energy how to be chosen to use in military strategies aspect or political aspect or economic diplomatic aspect. The country's leader will influence the whole country's social economy development in long term. However, individual and social stability are difficult to maintain in a social setting in which there is serious conflict between ethics and personal welfares. Because irrational honesty behaviour is usually caused between the personal welfare and ethics choice.

Can behavioral economy be applied to develop policy and influence economic growth effectively? Such policies stress that changing the way choices are presented or changing the environment in which decisions are made, can substantially alter behavior. Ideas from behavioral economics have helped to develop the traditional economic choice framework, in which people are assumed to make choices that are rational, self interested and consistent. Some of the most important behavioral insights for tax and benefit policy include: Faced with complicated decisions, people may make choices, which are often approximately optimal, in that who maximize welfare, but might in some cases lead to poor choices. There is evidence that how choices are presented affects outcomes.

The environment in which decisions are made would provide cues to make particular choices or made could provide cues to make particular choices, or some aspects of the choice problem may be more or less influence to consumers. When any policy relates to income and spending, or it is label money for another can affect what people choose to do with it. Individuals appear to care not just about their own outcomes, but also about those of others. This might be because people derive value from fairness and cooperation. These motivations could give intrinsic incentive to make particular choices. It is possible that providing extrinsic incentives, such as taxes, fines or rewards could be crowded our desirable behavior.

Consumers may have to exercise costly self control to make certain choices, such as eating health foods or giving up smoking. Commitment devices to help overcome self control problems are therefore values, for example, raising the cost of tempting choices, increasing cigarette taxes, say: when making choices with uncertain outcomes, people will do a number of behavioral features. Such as, attaching subjective decision weights to each outcome and these may differ from objective measures of probability. Usually, outcomes are measured against a reference point, relative to the reference point are felt more strongly than equivalent gains. When welfare increases and ever bigger gains falls, as the welfare cost is from ever bigger losses, then people will appear to be risk seekers when welfare cost comes to cause social loss. How people value the future changes with the passage of time. Usually people hope to earn immediate rewards in present than distant rewards in the future. This means that people make plans who find it hard to achieve. People may also make choices under the assumption that their preferences won't change in the future. So, for policymakers those biases have important implications for why behavior change interventions may be necessary.

Behavioral insights provide new reasons to intervene, issues of self control, for example, making failure, where outcomes are come from the perspective of either individuals or society or both usually. As a common failure is the case of externalities, when individual choices generate costs or benefits for others. Since, these are not taken into account in private decision making, which are come from a social perspective, there is too much or too little of the activity.

In this case, taxes or subsidies can help private and social incentives. So, behavioral economical concept can be suggested these important insights for externalities, such as private decisions are closer to the social optimum, reducing the need for correcting taxes or subsidies. It seems that taxes or subsidies will affect to change people's behaviors if social preferences are important. Externalities can arise not just because of how someone affects the well being of others, but also through how decisions made today affect the individual in the future. This is known as an internality. Taxes or subsidies policies both can influence people's present behaviors to be changed and future behaviors will be influenced to be changed from whose present behaviors in societies. Thus, policymakers can not neglect this policy of method to attempt to solve any social challenge nowadays.

Finally, I shall explain why national leader's behavior can assist policy development. Behavioral economy is a science, includes psychology, economics, finance and sociology to understand human behavior and decision making. Behavioral economics recognizes that constraints in time and mental resources prevent us from optimally evaluating every decision. To deal with our limitations, so we rely on mental decision to judge our face of uncertainty, but we can be leaded to predictably irrational behaviors from behavioral economical concept.

As government agencies enact laws and regulations that are focused in the society. They often rely on restrictions, incentives or public information campaigns in order to change citizen behavior. When well intentioned, those traditional approaches can be accepted. For example, regulations that can be supported to financial advisers disclose conflicts of interest have led to achieve any final results. Disclosures can increase pressures on advisees to comply with the advice provided and in some cases increase greater perceptions of trust rather than the evaluation of biased advice. Similarly, tax incentives can increase retirement savings rates which have had limited impact. Researchers studying the impact of concluded that such policies are an expensive way of encouraging new savings.

On the one hand, governments ought engage their citizens to do any action, whose action is influenced by behavioral economics to discover how behavioral economics can be provided powerful insights into human motivation and behavior. As different countries' government experiments are more from academic laboratories to the real world. So, it is a kind of method to be applied to assist any countries' governments how to use effective policy to improve people's lives. For example, designing what is the best reasonable taxes, subsidies, incentives or educational campaigns level at the rate, donations and retirement savings rates as well as healthy food product label consumption of selection etc. strategic policies which are related how to apply behavioral economy to analyze or experiment to gain the better choice among of them.

On the another hand, Economic agents ought attempt to spend time to gather data to choose to do the best decision, but not perfectly national ones. Also economic research should be used reasonable assumptions about agents' cognitive actives. So, economic models should take predictions that are consistent with micro-level data on decisions, including experimental evidence. Moreover, economists ought spend much time to learn from psychologists. Behavioral economists now routinely combine experimental data, field data and theory to construct their arguments. As behavioral economic continues to gain acceptance, behavioral economists will increasingly find themselves participating in policy discussions. As policy has the ability to do good or to create great mislead, depending on who, leader is in charge of making the rules. Indeed in some cases the findings of behavioral economists suggest that active policies may be quite harmful. Successful policy analysis should be concerned the motives of private actors, e.g. consumers and firms and the public or governmental actors need to design formulate and enforce policy with cooperation to regulators, bureaucrats, politicians.

So, policy analysis must also be carefully concerned the institutional environment in which these private and public actors interact, e.g. , market, elections and bureaucracies. However, any bad decision making is caused from bounded rationality, slow learning, framing and lack of self control with those effects in mind, one might conclude that government can easily improve consumers' welfare by paternalistically helping consumers make better decisions. Such paternalistic policies can improve consumer welfare by enhancing an individual's maximizing whose own welfare. So, this stands in contrast to most public policies, which address externalities or public products problems that arise because of interactions among economic agents.

To conclude, national leader and whose psychology which can influence whether he can do the reasonable policy and which have close relationship, As if the national leader had health psychology, then who will have more possible to achieve good behavior to perform to decide how to achieve any the best public policies to raise growth to make welfare to whose citizens.

So any policymakers ought need to concern how to listen to behavioral scientists to let them to give any recommendation how to improve or review or revise whose psychological challenges to let them have more effort to decide how to choose to do the right decision effectively. Because the relationship between psychology and behavioral science has more generally to influence public policy which is particularly painful and frustrating of the success for any similar policy recommendations. Hence, economics and psychology indeed can provide policymakers with vital tools to develop the best policy to solve any social challenges.

Consequently, it seems the leader's psychology will influence whose behavioral performance to be decided to choose to do the more correct policy to influence economic development more easily. It also means that one leader's psychology is an important factor to influence any social economic development directly for long term. So who can not neglect to concern whether whose psychological mind is right or wrong to already to make any decisions to plan any policies before whose any polices are implemented. Because the leader's psychology will influence whose behavior is more correct to decide to decide how to do any policies effectively.

On conclusion, if we hope our future living to be improved, we need follow as several aspects in order to raise our economic growth more easily. Then we will build best between living standard and economic growth.

Reference

Dimson, Marsh & Staunton, London Business School (2005) In The Global Investment Returns Year Book, ABN Amro.

Fiscal Policy And Long Term Growth, International Monetary Fund, IMF policy papers, Washington, D.C. Available from April, 2015, http://www.imf.org/external/pp/ppindex.aspx

reference

Schmokler, J. (1966). Invention and economic growth, Harvard University Press, Cambridge , Mass.

CHAPTER TWO

Information technological environment impacts consumption desires change

● Behavioral and environmental economic prediction to traveler and energy user behavior in information technological environment

How and why can we apply environmental and behavioral economic methods to predict consumer behaviors? Environment and economics has close relationship to influence consumer behaviors. For example, one of the prime reasons for climate change, global warmth factor influences energy consumer's , e.g. householder, drivers, business office energy users etc. different stakeholders useful behaviors at home, offices, driving etc. different modes of energy uses. Because human begins to feel environment protection needs to avoid to use waste of energy in any time. It has a link between the burning of fossil fuels and global warming relationship to impact human how uses natural resource energy every day. It means that reducing energy to use to avoid global warmth crisis to bring threat for the environment protection energy users. So, their energy consumption desire will be also influenced to reduce, e.g. driving less vehicle, turning off home light when the householder feels that he does not need to turn on light, turn on fans, turn on air conditions etc. electricity waste behaviors at homes. For example, US energy users begin to feel energy waste will bring global warmth negative effect in possible to influence their daily lives to be worse. They have predicted that, should global temperatures continue to increase, within decades the polar ice-caps could melt, potentially raising sea levels, around the world and flooding major including New York, London. Further feared outcomes include the shutdown of the Gulf Stream across the Atlantic, which some claim could seriously disrupt the climate in Northern

Europe. So, many US people and UK people begin to avoid to waste to use any energy at homes, at offices, less time to drive cars on roads etc. different kinds of energy useful behaviors in energy consumption view.

According to Sir Nicholas Stern, a UK economist who authored one of the first reports on the eventual costs associated with climate change could mount to around 20% of global gross domestic product, around $6 trillion compared with costs of just 1 % of GDP to tackle the threat now. So, environment production energy consumers will reduce to waste much energy daily and it will influence the energy consumption GDP income to reduce to any countries in the future. It is only technological innovation can be applied to help human to avoid global warming in possible if one day , new technological innovation can be invented to avoid global warming, then the energy consumption GDP income will have increasing chance because the environment protection consumers won't feel waste energy consumption to bring global warming crisis and they will accept to increase energy use again in daily living in possible. For example, during Victorian times in London, one of the main fears of the population was the concern that as the city grew, and with it the number of horses on the streets, the English capital would eventually become buried in a pile of horse manure, such as outcome never transpired because of the birth of the motor car (new technological driving tool invention). Similarly, there is much evidence to suggest that new technologies, whether hydrogen-powered motor cars, nuclear –fusion generators or carbon –capture facilities to allow clean burning of coal, will help solve the crisis without subtracting significant economic growth from today's generation. So, if scientists can invent one kind of environment protection energy to let human to use, then human will accept to use much this kind of energy to instead other kinds of pollution energies and the GDP on energy income will also raise in possible.

Hence, climate change is an example of market failure. It is the worst market failure to influence any energy users' daily energy useful behaviors to be changed to less energy consumption behaviors. In a properly functioning market, the price of something goes up when its supply falls or demand for it rises, this is a key element of the invisible hand theory. So, when human feels that more waste to use energy , this waste energy useful behavior can bring environment pollution more seriously , then it will bring the energy demand is reduced and it will influence energy price goes down because demand is less and supply will also need to reduce as the same time in economic view point. However, because until very recently there was no price put on either fresh air or pollution how have relationship to influence energy price variable to less in energy consumption market. But, the actual implied cost of pollution is very high, if pollution caused more desertification and higher sea levels, any lays waste to towns and cities, it will come at a great price variable influence to energy consumption market. But, it is only since scientists realized the potential of climate change for environment pollution influence to prove that they have possible relationship to waste energy useful effect. In theory, the price of combating climate change ought to be what people are willing to pay in order to ensure that they and their children have clean air and water in the future. So, environment protection people will reduce to waste to use energy to avoid this issue occurrence.

How and why behavioral economics can predict consumers' daily behaviors change. Experience shows that people are by no means consistently rational. Such as one smoker will reduce to smoke suddenly, the reasons may include health factor, air pollution factor, cigarettes price increasing factor, income reducing factor, living habit changing factor, family and friend bad relationship factor to influence whose smoking behavior. So, their emotion will be influenced to be poor and it can bring the smokers' smoking behavior changes to be influenced to less smoking. It is good example to make them act irrationally.

Behavioral economic investigates why and how people act irrationally. It is among the newest and most fascinating are as of academic study, combining economics and psychology and it is an understanding develops as to how the mind and the brain work, so behavioral economists are providing greater insight into what really drives people to act.I shall explain economists can apply behavioral and environmental economic to predict energy consumers' behavioral changing as below:

If the economic process consists of temporarily re-arranging some of the earth's resources, energy is what brings about the characteristics that change of scope. Nowadays, human begins to feel where the use of the world energy has become careless, such as drought and the energy crisis. Although this issue is not tangible commodity, but this issue can let human to feel the worse pollution brings to air and water pollution, drought natural environment damage if we still waste to use energy daily.

To understand the role of energy how acts in economic process. I indicate this example, for one farmer , he has arranged the scope of his economic process in such as a way that he requires energy in high density forms. The reason is fundamentally that he requires much of it for eventual transformation into motion, whether for transport or in fixed installations. The farmer concern how he use energy for his farming activity which it is easily carried either with him in his hand farming tool using or farming agriculture machine tool using method. It needs to be in a concentrated and tangible form to choose either of one method. Whether the farmer consider the environment pollution issue if he use any farming machines to replace hand tools to work in agricultural daily tasks aspect. If the farmer feels that farming machine can bring air pollution more easily, then he will choose to do farming tasks by hand, although he feels hard and spend long time to do farming tasks, but he can protect our earth to be polluted by the dirty air. So, energy need must be reduced when the farmer decides not to use farming machines to work on much time., even he does not choose to use farming machine to work on farm. Consequently, oil or electricity need will reduce to the farmer. It is one good example how air pollution influences energy consumers' behavior.

Then, environment pollution will also influence energy suppliers' market behavior changes, e.g. when they discovered that oil or electricity demand is less, then they will reduce supply number to keep price does not need to reduce or goes down prices if they still keep the same oil or electricity suppling level in economic supply and demand theory. They need to make the better decisions on how to reduce the oil or electricity supplying level to avoid the price reducing result. So, the environment pollution issue will influence the oil, electricity suppliers' price changes and supplying number changes in possible. Hence, behavioral economic view, it also explain that environment pollution can influence economic organizations need react in predictably irrational ways when they feel that environment pollution issue is the important factor to influence oil and electricity need to be reduced at the moment.

Moreover, energy shortage will influence products need, such as car industry. Because oil or gas will have shortage problem. When scientists do not real invent another new energy to instead them to use on cars. But, since the electric cars invention, it can replace the traditional cars, it can use electricity to replace oil and gas resource and it is one kind of environmental protection new energy to reduce air pollution. SO, when global drivers can accept to drive electric cars on roads , then the electrical cars need will also increase and its supply will also increase in global vehicle industry. So, the electricity need will also increase when one day global cars are used by electrical energy. So, environment pollution issue can also influence car manufacturers choose to manufacture many electric cars to prepare to sell if they believe that artificial intelligent or non manual driving and electric cars are accepted to drive on roads in popular. Although, electric cars prices are not cheap nowadays, but when human feel global warming, air pollution crisis will damage our natural environment and cause food shortage crisis. Then, electric cars number will not be influenced to demand less ,even its price is higher than traditional oil energy form cars. So, the inelastic price change will be future electric cars market characteristics. I suppose that electric car buyers will not be an irrational decision buyers in common.

Moreover, environment pollution will influence travelers travelling needs because when one traveler feel that his travelling times and long journey number can influence air pollution when the air plane needs much oils or gas energy to fly long time on sky. Then, the environment pollution awareness can influence his catching long time flying number to be reduced. Consequently, the airlines' freight travelling journey time and flying number will also reduce when many travelers begin to reduce to choose long journey and reduce travelling number. Then, the oil or gas needs on airline will reduce , even the oil and gas price will also reduce because oil and gas demand on airlines industry , it is reduced. If the oil or gas supplier does not hope to reduce price , due to the oil or gas demand on airlines is reduced, it can choose to reduce the supply to airlines . Hence, on environmental and behavioral economic view, environmental pollution may influence oil/gas suppliers' income and it can change any consumers who need to apply oil or gas energy to enjoy their entertainment activities to change to less really.

- Household energy use: Applying behavioural economics to understand consumer decision-making and behaviour

Household energy conservation has emerged as a major challenge and opportunity for researchers, practitioners and policymakers. Consumers also seem to be gaining greater awareness of the value and need for sustainable energy practices, particularly amid growing public concerns over greenhouse gas emissions and climate change. Adequate knowledge of how to save energy and a professed desire to do so, many consumers still fail to take noticeable steps towards energy efficiency and conservation. There is often a sizeable discrepancy between peoples' self-reported knowledge, values, attitudes and intentions, and their observable behaviour—examples include the well-known 'knowledge-action gap' and 'value-action gap'. But neither is household energy consumption driven primarily by financial incentives and the rational pursuit of material interests. In fact, people sometimes respond in unexpected and undesirable ways to rewards and sanctions intended to shift consumers' cost–benefit calculus in favour of sustainable behaviours. Why is household energy consumption and conservation difficult to predict from either core values or material interests? By drawing on critical insights from behavioural economics and psychology, we illuminate the key cognitive biases and motivational factors that may explain why energy-related behaviour with either the personal values or material interests of consumers. Understanding these psychological phenomena can make household and community responses to public policy interventions and it can help us design more cost-effective and mass-scalable behavioural solutions to encourage renewable and sustainable energy use among consumers.

Consumer behaviour is complex and rarely follows traditional economic theories of decision-making. When choosing what products to buy or what services to use, people often think they are making smart decisions and behaving in ways that are highly rational and congruent with their values and intentions. However, in daily life, people routinely deviate from the 'rational choice' model of human behaviour, in which one objectively weighs up the costs and benefits of all alternatives before choosing the optimal course of action. But neither is human decision-making reliably predicted by what people know is the 'best' or feel is the 'right' thing to do. For example, so-called 'green' knowledge and values – such as knowing about or feeling positive towards the use of renewable resources, sustainable products, low-emission technology, public transportation, and so forth – do not reliably translate into pro-environmental choices when buying goods or using services that impact the environment. Many people still rely heavily on non-renewable resources, under-use public transport, fail to recycle, and engage in other everyday actions that harm or neglect the environment—actions they may themselves acknowledge as 'wasteful' Even consumers who face strong material incentives, and/or possess knowledge and motivation patently sufficient to act in more sustainable ways, may struggle to shift their behaviour in the desired direction, particularly over the longer term.

To understand why and how pollution influences energy consumer useful behavior. First, it is clear we need to know what people say and what they do are sometimes very different things. In many domains of human behaviour, we see a knowledge-action gap. For example, people may know about, intrinsically value, hold positive attitudes towards, and/or genuinely intend to act in some socially desirable way. Yet often these things do not translate into actual behaviour. One domain of consumer behaviour where this disjuncture is evident is residential energy use. Many people report that they are concerned about climate change and understand the importance of saving energy, yet this concern does not reliably translate into taking ongoing, practical steps to reduce household energy consumption. It is perhaps unsurprising, then, that traditional education programmes and mass media campaigns – which strive to promote pro-environmental knowledge and attitudes by simply disseminating information.

At the same time, it is also clear that people's behaviour does not generally fall short of their environmental concerns and commitments simply because they are pursuing material interests and extrinsic rewards. Even where energy-saving measures are demonstrably cost-effective (e.g., insulation, low-carbon technology) – making uptake of the technology or behaviour economically rational for the consumer – many people remain reluctant to introduce these things into their lives and homes. In fact, offering extrinsic rewards and financial incentives to encourage pro-social behaviour (e.g., volunteering, reciprocity, civic duty, charitable donations, or other 'public good' contributions), presumably by prompting more favourable cost–benefit appraisals, can sometimes backfire and decrease the desired behaviour by 'crowding out' intrinsic motivation to act altruistically.Though not reliably predicted by either environmental concerns or material interests, individual choices around pro-environmental behaviour and resource consumption are, in fact, predictable—. As with much of human behaviour, energy-related practices are often influenced by certain cognitive biases and 'irrational' tendencies that, while producing decisions and actions that may be surprising from the standpoint of traditional economic models, are actually rather predictable (and even adaptive/functional) from the perspective of psychology and behavioural economics.

● Applying psychology and behavioural economics to explain, predict and change consumer behaviour

Traditional economic theory postulates that human decision-making and behaviour are based on purely rational choice . More recent neoclassical economic approaches also rest on several fundamental assumptions aligned with rational choice theoy, that people have rational preferences among outcomes, always strive to maximise utility, and act independently based on full and relevant information. Based on these assumptions, traditional economic models predict that people will make decisions that yield the optimal result given budget constraints, and that behavioural choices can be improved by providing people with more information (i.e., by increasing knowledge/awareness) and/or more options (i.e., by increasing choices).

In contrast to such assumptions, a growing body of scientific research demonstrates that people are rarely the rational decision-makers envisaged by traditional economic models of human behaviour. Empirical evidence from psychology and behavioural economics shows that consumer choices and actions often deviate systematically from neoclassical economic assumptions of rationality, and there are certain fundamental and persistent biases in human decision-making that regularly produce behaviour that these assumptions cannot account for. Hence, to understanding energy consumption, especially in terms of predicting and changing the behaviour of individuals and households. Among the most powerful and pervasive biases to influence consumers' patterns of energy usage include the status quo bias, loss and risk aversion, sunk-cost effects, temporal and spatial discounting, and the availability bias. In parallel, psychological phenomena such as normative social influence, intrinsic and extrinsic rewards, and trust may also play a key role. A large body of research shows that even where cost–benefit calculations would suggest more materially advantageous choices, people persist in displaying seemingly irrational. For example, people tend to resist change and 'go with the flow' of pre-set options, even where alternatives may yield better (e.g., more financially rewarding or materially advantageous) personal or collective outcomes. Providing a default not only saves people time (by relieving them of having to make an active choice), but it might also be viewed as the best option (since it is apparently being 'recommended' by the provider. Evidence of this status quo bias has been observed across a range of experimental and applied contexts, including residential energy consumption. For another example, people typically process only enough information to reach a satisfactory decision rather than processing all available information to reach an optimal decision, as the latter demands much more time, effort and resources than would ordinarily seem justified by the prospective increase in utility or satisfaction. Yet this tendency to settle for 'good enough' may come at a price, with people often making worse decisions and poorer choices (or avoiding action altogether) when faced with more information and/or options.

Energy useful consumers can feel to avoid loss averse by weighing losses more heavily than equal-sized gains, particularly as the stakes rise. For example, people typically focus on the risks, costs or losses associated with adopting a new behaviour, such as financial costs (what will it cost me?), physical risks (is it safe/healthy?), social costs (what do others think?), ecological risks (is it environmentally friendly?), time costs (will it take longer?), functional risks (does it fit my routine?), and even psychological costs (how will I feel?), and tend to discount equivalent gains and benefits. When faced with making a decision, people perceive the disutility of losing something as far greater than the utility of gaining something (i.e., they feel the pain of losses far more than the pleasure of gains). This tendency is reflected by contingent valuation studies that show that willingness to accept tends to be higher than willingness to pay.

Energy useful consumers tend to become irrationally fixated on 'recovering' losses already suffered, discounting future costs and benefits. Once time, effort or money has been invested in a particular endeavour, they may persist with that course of action and 'throw good money after bad' even as it becomes riskier or increasingly unlikely to yield the desired result. Some researchers have attributed this tendency to an overgeneralisation of the 'Don't waste' rule that many people have learned during childhood, i.e., the notion that avoiding waste is generally advisable, so abandoning a prior investment may seem to 'waste' the resources already expended . In the residential energy domain, for instance, a consumer who outlays time, effort and money to purchase an electrical appliance (e.g., air conditioner, extra refrigerator) may tend to use it more, even when it is not necessarily required. The perceive things as less valuable or significant if further away in time (temporal discounting) or space (spatial discounting), even if such things afford long-term benefits. For example, people often 'discount the future' by preferring smaller immediate rewards (e.g., $5 now) over larger future rewards (e.g., $10 next year), and they may avoid actions that are costly in the short-term (e.g., outlaying time and money to purchase new energy-efficient appliances or making an effort to switch energy retailers), despite offering longer-term benefits (e.g., reduced electricity bills). This tendency to be short-sighted and make time-inconsistent judgements often leads to procrastination, inertia and decreased cooperation in group settings.

Energy consumers can be motivated by rewards and incentives, both intrinsic (e.g., achieving social equity/fairness, the 'warm glow' of acting altruistically) and extrinsic (e.g., money) [. In general, larger incentives or disincentives lead to greater behavioural responses . However, the effects of financial incentives are often surprisingly short-lived and/or inconsistent, with behaviour reverting back to baseline levels upon removal of the reward. People may even respond negatively to extrinsic rewards (e.g., showing loss of motivation, overjustification, moral licensing effects), particularly if intrinsic motivation for the target behaviour is already high8. For example, if a person is intrinsically motivated to be altruistic, giving a piece-rate monetary reward to incentivise the desired behaviour may have a counteractive effect by 'crowding out' the intrinsic motivation .For example, the efficacy of public awareness campaigns and informational appeals can often depend on the perceived credibility of the communication source . If the source of a message seems untrustworthy, unfair or incompetent, people can be wary or sceptical and either disengage, or react defensively to the information. For example, Gonzales et al. have suggested that when communicating messages to improve householders' energy efficiency (e.g., advocating retrofitting), framing recommendations in terms of loss (i.e., energy and money lost via inaction) rather than gain (i.e., energy or money gained via action) may be more effective. Thus, a statement such as, 'You are currently losing $20 per billing quarter by not switching off your lights' is likely to be more motivating than stating, 'You could save $20 per quarter by turning off your lights'. Likewise, stating, 'What you are currently doing is three times less efficient than doing x' is likely to be more motivating than, 'Doing x is three times more efficient than what you are currently doing'. However, various factors may moderate the motivational impact of a particular message frame (e.g., level of risk associated with target behaviour, who/what the reference point is, characteristics of target audience), and these should be taken into account to maximise the effectiveness of consumer-focused communication, particularly when tailoring messages to different customer segments.

Risk aversion: Focus on the low-risk of energy-saving practices and investments that are safe, stable and secure, particularly where energy-efficiency technology is new, expensive, or not yet mainstream. Uncertainty around electricity supply, market prices, government policies and long-term financial payoffs make investing in energy-saving products and services seem like a risky decision for many consumers , so marketing and communication to alleviate these perceived risks may increase energy-efficient action. Extensive research has examined the impact of different risk-reduction strategies ('risk relievers') on consumer behaviour, particularly in retail environments where perceived risk and uncertainty may prevent people from purchasing new products or services relevant to household energy efficiency and conservation are 'relievers' for financial risks (e.g., offering discounts, rebates, lowest-price and money-back guarantees, no-cost returns/refunds, payment security), time risks (e.g., making the purchase decision and product installation quick), and effort risks (e.g., simplified product design, 'user-friendly' operating instructions, helpful customer service). For example, offering consumers money-back guarantees on new energy-efficient technology (e.g., direct load control devices, smart meters) or obligation-free trials of new services (e.g., renewable or 'green' electricity) may increase consumer uptake by providing a 'safety net' – a sense of certainty and security – around any 'unknowns'. Other useful 'relievers' may include strategies to reduce perceived risks around product/service performance and functionality (e.g., offering free trials/samples, demonstrations, guarantees, extended warranties, free product installation and/or training), physical and safety risks (e.g., providing instructions, expert advice, safety certification, independent testing), the risk of product obsolescence (e.g., promising free or low-cost upgrades, product compatibility with earlier versions), social risks (e.g., securing positive word-of-mouth, customer testimonials, celebrity or expert endorsements, or promoting products or services as popular or socially desirable), and even psychological risks (e.g., building brand credibility, customer loyalty).

On conclusion, to ensure cost-effectiveness and maximise return on investment, it is important to take these phenomena into account when developing strategies for encouraging renewable and sustainable energy use, and for motivating pro-environmental behaviour more broadly. By understanding these predictable deviations from economically rational behaviour, policymakers will be better placed to craft interventions that successfully bridge the gap between pro environmental knowledge, values, attitudes and intentions, and the everyday energy-related behaviour of consumers. This paper has highlighted the value of applying insights from psychology and behavioural economics to inform the effective design and delivery of consumer-focused communication, messages, and other behavioural interventions aimed at encouraging household energy conservation. So, the impact of haze pollution on residents' green consumption behavior is explored to influence energy consumers behaviors.

I shall indicate Chinese energy users example to expain how pollution influence their energy consumption behavior. At present, Chinese residents have been suffering from the influence of air pollution, especially haze pollution. However, residents‘ consumption is also one of the main sources of haze pollution. Therefore, residents’ green consumption can reduce haze pollution. This paper is to explore the impact of haze pollution on residents‘ green consumption behavior. Shandong Province is taken as the illustrative case to carry on the empirical analysis. Firstly, the grounded theory is used to develop the residents’ green consumption behavior model affected by haze pollution. Secondly, based on the data obtained by investigation, the structural equation model is used to test the theoretical model. Finally, the hierarchical regression model is utilized to study the moderating effect of situational variables on residents' green consumption behavior. The green consumption willingness (GCW) has a significant positive driving effect on green consumption behavior. Furthermore, the haze pollution perception (HPP) plays the most positive role in promoting green consumption willingness, followed by behavioral constrain (BC) and haze mitigation responsibility (HMR). Among all situational variables, the government incentive (IM) has a positive moderating effect on the relationship between green consumption willingness and invested green consumption behavior (IGCB). However, publicity and education activities (PEA) have a reverse moderating effect on the relationship between green consumption willingness and invested green consumption behavior. The difference of the impact of age, income, occupation and household structure on habitual green consumption behavior (HGCB) is significant. However, there are significant differences in the effects of age, income, and educational background on invested green consumption behavior. According to the results received in this paper, more policy recommendations are presented.

As we are entering a new age where industrialization, trades, technology development, and resource exploitation are at their peak, the economy and average income, together with social development have had impressive progresses, while our environment is facing serious problems such as different kinds of pollution and large amount of energy consumption that is almost draining the currently scarce resource, threatening the further development of human beings from communities to countries and even to the globe as a whole

As the environment is getting more and more vulnerable and polluted, the health of people is seriously harmed and many important industries, for example, agriculture, fishing, astronomy, the development of micro machines, transportation, and even building constructions and designations, are also heavily affected due to the significant drop of available resources and the heavy pollution of the air, water, and plantations, sometimes even the changes in climates . The existing problems are getting more and more severe, harming the health of people, blocking the economic development, causing instability among societies, threatening humanity.

However, while much of the pollution emitted and energy used are necessary for human development, for example, fossil fuels and industrial wastes that are necessary to keep the economy going, a lot of energy consumption and pollution are actually unnecessary and are caused by the psychological biases of people, which, if reduced, can strongly mitigate the environmental problems we are facing . So, apart from pure technological development that directly solves the environmental problems by ways like creating more resources or purifying the polluted Earth, etc., methods involving insights from Behavioral Economics that drive people to be greener can also be a focus of our efforts in solving the environmental problems, which can both save large amount of money for individuals, corporations, and even governments, and provide us with a suitable environment for living, working, and developing

Hence, China government needs to impletment many actions have already been taken by different organizations and governments, most having a considerable influence and certain benefits. Many ideas have also been proposed . All of the existing solutions and their results can serve as desirable references for those who are intending to solve the problems. However, since the situations vary from place to place and the solutions working at one place might not be as effective as expected in another, it is relatively hard to come to a specific universal solution for the high level of pollution and energy consumption.

Regarding the problems caused by the status quo biases, which cause people to be unwilling to purchase eco-friendly products that cost at first but save money gradually simply because they feel an irrational appeal to the current product, the government can set up some sort of incentives to offset the unwillingness to change. For example, a factory will be more than happy to change the original equipment into new, eco-friendly one if they receive money or fewer bills for doing so. The same also works with the problems caused by "discounting the future". While people tend to focus more on the immediate benefit, an upfront inventive can never be resisted. Just as the "Green Deal" has done, the government can give incentives in a way of cutting (or even eliminating) the upfront costs of installing green products and get the installing cost back in the following period of time as a little amount of extra charge that is still less than the predicted cost of the original product, which can attract tons of people. Because, facing a large amount of energy consumption saved by installing those products with no upfront cost, everyone gets it that it saves both money and the environment without any cost.

Incentives can also work for the problems of "doubt". For example, one might be more willing to purchase an electric car if it is cheaper, or if it saves the user much more money, of which the value exceeds the "risk" of using a "dangerous product" in the consumer's mind. Incentives can be given in many different ways. I can be given straight to the individuals that contribute to the green work. It can also be given to a certain community to take advantage of group spirits, encouraging communities to produce less pollution, for example, carrying out garbage classification, using less air conditioning, driving more eco-friendly cars, using less water and electricity, or producing less waste, or using less plastic bags, with promised incentives, which can cause people behave in the way we expect because of their eagerness to bring the benefits to both themselves and the people within their own communities And while everyone in a community is doing the eco-friendly things, one will be more likely to carry out the same things due to the "social influences", which adds to the effectiveness of the incentives and provides oversights for the people, since everyone wants the incentives and will be watching those around him or her and make sure they are also doing the things needed to get the incentives for the whole community. Incentives can be given as money. Incentives can also be given as a gift, for example, a meal for free, a phone for free, or even several paid days off. And they can even be given as some sort of discounts at certain stores. Since different forms of incentives have their attraction for different groups of people, the diversity of the forms of incentives should be appreciated. While proper incentives encourage people to be green, several improper incentives might not have such great outcomes. Giving too many incentives might lead to losses for the government or the related companies that outweighs the benefits generated by being greener. And giving incentives that are too small might not have a desirable effect since a lot of people just do not care about the "small stuff". And proper forms of incentives are essential for attracting certain groups of people. So, when deciding to use incentives to deal with the problems, policy-makers have to weigh the benefits and risks and think carefully. Researches are also required to make a wise decision. Hence, incentive is one good method to solve pollution when people consumes energy to use in any time.

CHAPTER THREE

Information economy how influences our society

Nowadays, we will contact different information from different sources, e.g. internet, newspaper, magazine, radio, television. So, our daily lives are influenced by any information and we will analyze the useful information to do any decision, e.g. consumption, entertainment, travelling, learning etc. So, information can influence our societies to develop. However, I believe that , due to internet invention can be applied to mobile invention. Hence, human feel mobile is not only phone call function, it can be applied to link internet to find any data from website in any where and in any time conveniently. I shall indicate some cases to explain how and why internet information can influence mobile to help us to gather any data to do any decisions in any where and any time . So, mobile will bring more influence to our future economy development, I shall explain as below:

Economic science has a direct impact on our lives and it has a critical role to play to consumers and organization decision makers. Such as when you read the newspapers about disputes concerning current economic issue, are you often argue the issue? If you think that a better, cheaper television information source does come from newspapers, radio, television or magazine advertisement, then what channel that you will gather the kind of television information, internet will be the best channel to gather information because it is rapid and convenient. So, technological innovation can influence consumers to gather information. Any people can turn on computer and we can find any information from internet. It is one the lowest cost and less time spending information gather method. Every aspect of human behavior reacts to cost in some way. When the cost of something fall, becomes more attractive to use. Such as internet information gather channel method. But, how internet information gathering channel influences our economic development, instead of human information gathering behavior changes.

For a firm case, when it can attempt to sell the same item to different consumers at different prices. (price discrimination). When you are on an airplane, ask the person next to you how much he or she paid for the ticket. It's probably nor what you paid. You are sitting on the same plane, travelling to the same destination, eating the same food on the plan, but your both ticket price may be difference. Because you do not apply internet to compare the ticket price or you do not apply internet to gather the item price to decide to buy the firm product. So, such as air ticket consumer or product consumer to you, because you do not spend little time to gather air ticket price or the product price information to ensure whether you make decision to buy the product or pre paid the air ticket is reasonable at the moment. If you can gather their information to make decision from internet. It is possible that you do not like to pay for them. So, internet role is one fair or reasonable price gathering tool to let consumers to make compare in order to decide to buy any thing. If any consumers apply internet to gather price information. Then, their sale income will reduce when their prices are unreasonable higher to compare normal days. Consequently, there are not many consumers decide to buy their any things. So, their prices increasing chance will be less , if they hope consumers buy their products easily nowadays. It implies that internet can change consumer behaviors to be clever consumers more than foolish consumers nowadays. Also, it means that firms are not acting in their own best interests more easily because internet creates. For example, when one traveler gather information concerns whether it is less cost between catching air plane or driving car to arrive the destination in US. He can gather information from internet more easily. Using a car seat requires that a family buy an extra seat on the plane, which dramatically increases the cost of flying when he find the domestic plane ticket price information from internet. Airlines no longer offer significant children's discount, a seat is a scat, and it is likely to cost more dollars. As a result, some families will choose to drive rather than fly in US.

Information message delivery invention can bring some product sale number , even price increase, e.g. mobile phone can be popular to use for call phone, it can also be used for internet , word message delivery function in public places, such as restaurants and commuter trains, even vehicles, instead of homes. So, high information technological product invention and human needs to receive and deliver any messages in short time rapidly, these two factors influence mobile phone demand number increases, even it can be used to replace computers when some consumers feel it can have internet function. It is one kind substitute product to replace laptop in possible our future message delivery process. So, information can bring mobile phone product innovation need in order to satisfy consumers phone call and internet useful needs. It also bring mobile phone need increases. It is another kind of information product to influence our social and economic development because any people can apply mobile phone to gather information from internet, instead of computers.

Information society also changes student learning behavior because students can choose to study from distance learning as well as they can apply internet to ask email to enquire teachers any questions and teachers can also send email to answer their questions by email response rapidly. It will bring traditional school classroom education to change online education. ON economic benefit aspect, online education can bring none classroom long time listening need to students, reducing transportation costs, school fees and long teaching time, teacher number can be reduced when every teacher can apply internet to teach 10, 20 or more students in the same time from internet channel. Online education can bring learning time reduces, cost reduces, teaching employees number reduces to school teachers and students both. It will bring long time social economic benefit when schools do not need classroom, they do not need to spend more money to build any school buildings , e.g. library, classroom. They can apply internet to let students to borrow books or read electronic books well as apply internet to discuss between students or enquire questions between teachers. So, cost and learning and teaching time is reduced absolutely when online education is accepted in popular.

Information society brings benefit to raise productivity and improve human capital. Economists study poverty and income inequality. They seek to understand who is poor, why they are poor, and what can be done about it. Human capital is the sum total of skills within an individual: education, intelligence, creativity, work experience, entrepreneurial mind. The labor market is no different from the market of anything, some kinds of talent are in greater demand than others.

Nowadays, internet can help any foolish people to learn any new knowledge rapidly. It can help any organizations to raise productivity, e.g. when one team workers can apply internet to enter their organization's website to learn the steps how to finish their tasks at home. So, the organization do not need trainer trains them in workshop or working places. Its employees can learn any working related skills from itself company website conveniently. When they feel difficult, they can send email to ask the trainer and the trainer can also send to answer their enquiries form internet rapidly. So, internet can attempt to solve the income inequality and poverty problem. It can help the foolish workers to raise productive efficiency in short time when they attempt to apply internet to learn any new skills or working related knowledge to prepare their employers' working demand or the job seekers can attempt to learn any new skills to prepare to satisfy their new employers' tasks demand in short time. Even employees can apply internet to work at home if their employers have online working chance. So, they do not need to spend long time to catch public transport tools to go to offices and they need 9 to 10 hours to work in offices every day. They can choose to work from their company's website on to two days or more every week conveniently. Even, some organizations won't need offices because they apply internet channel to let their employees to work at home. So, they do not need to pay rent and electricity expenditure. Online working model can help them to reduce much essential expenditure nowadays. For example, when one China employee can apply internet to do whose America employer tasks at China home town. So, he does not need to buy air ticket to fly to US to work , he does not need to rent house to live in US when this China employee can apply internet to work in China. So, internet working channel reduces this China employee's working time, because he can apply his private to work any time when he can stay at himself China home to apply internet to work for his US employer. It can good economic benefits to this US employer and this China employee when this US employer can accept internet is one kind of working channel to let its overseas employee to stay in his country to work at home.

So, internet working channel can help organizations to raise productivity growth when it depends on internet working channel on investment in physical capital, its company website is such as office to let their employees to work and they can send their tasks or assignment by email to their supervisors when they finish every day immediately; internet can help foolish or low skilled employees to raise their learning level because they can apply internet to find any information to learn their working related knowledge conveniently at home. Then they can improve performance because they are one talent employee after they learn any working related knowledge from internet rapidly.

Information society can improve organization performance and productivity to be raised. Our economy is changing to the high information online working model from the traditional office working model on economic benefit view. Our economy is evolving in ways in nearly that favor skills workers. For example, the shift toward computer skills in nearly every industry favors workers who either have computer skills or are smart enough to learn them on the job. Technology makes smart workers more productive when making low-skilled workers redundant. ATMs replaced bank tellers, self-serve pumps replaced gas station attendants, automated assembly lines replaced workers doing mindless, repetitive tasks. Indeed, assembly lines at General Motors , changed the major trend in the American economy. Computers and sophisticated robots now assemble the major components of a car, which creates high-paying jobs for people who write software and design robots when reducing the demands for workers with no specialized skills other than a willingness to do an honest day's work. So, high technological information society creates many high skilled occupations to let talent people to work. e.g. artificial intelligence innovation will improve employee performance and productivities to the best in our future.

However, information technological economic development also brings disadvantage to some people. When the country only accept talent people to work, then the foolish people will feel difficult to find jobs in societies. For Microsoft founder, Bill Gates, he indicated that he did not stand in the way of their success or benefit from their misfortunes. Rather, his vision and talent created an amount of wealth that nor everybody got to share really. There is a crucial distinction between a world I which Bill Gates gets rich by stealing other people's crops and a world I which he gets rich by growing his own food supply, such as Microsoft products that he shares with some people and others. The latter is a better representation of how a modern economy works. So, he means that human must need to continue to invent any new technology in order to attempt to help our society to innovate successfully, e.g. mobile phone product invention, laptop invention, non-manual driven vehicle, robotic invention for working aspect, learning aspect, driving aspect, flying aspect, shopping center or security etc. different future social needs. So, it is fact that talent people e.g. high skill software inventors , they will be needed to increase more to compare foolish people, e.g. low skill workers. Although, the gap between high salary and low salary between them , it will increase. But, if our future society can not achieve to manufacture any high information technological innovation or product invention to satisfy any organizations , such as office, factory, public transport, library etc. different artificial intelligence manufactory or service needs to satisfy customer needs as well as ourselves private needs, e.g. non manual driving need, robotic teaching and learning need etc. different personal living needs. Then, our society will not change to be raised and improved to our living standard significantly. Hence, if we hope our real economic growth, we must encourage any new information technological continue to develop further. Otherwise, our future social economy will not real grow to manufacturing , service , entertainment , education etc. different industries in our future.

● The relationship between information technological development and economic development

Can information technological development bring economic growth? Does information technological development raise the unemployment ratio when the low skillful workers are replaced by the high skillful workers? Can information technological development raise GDP income or increase high technological products sale number? Can information technological development change consumer desires to choose to increase to buy high technological products, e.g.
any artificial intelligent related manufacturing products to use by householder, factory or office workers,
drivers, at home, office, warehouse, shopping center, transportation etc. different places. How information technological development impact our future daily lives? I shall attempt to indiate some cases to explain how any why information technological development and our future lives and economy growth
which have close relationship as below:

It is not an oversimplification to say that the popular media, e.g. internet can provide online book publishers
to sell electronic books to let readers to read from online, such as Amazon publish. This ebooks publisher can let
readers to read electronic books from internet. So, some paper book readers will be influenced to change their
reading habit to read e-books. It means that traditional paper book publishers will face e-book publishers to competition.

In this global reading market. It is one good example, information technological development has change readers' reading habit or change their reading interest from paper books reading habit to electronic books reading habit nowadays. In the future, it is possible to occur that none any paper books to study, all readers need to apply internet to read any newspapers,magazines, ebooks. Then, due to ebooks reading model is popular to accept to many paper books readers. Many paper book publishers will close their businesses because competition is very serious. IN global, it is only ebook publishers can exist in global publishing market. The publishing industry will be grown or it can increase GDP income when every ebook reader

change ebook reading habit to bring unlimited royalties to ebooks authors and e-book publishers. It is possible to occur within 10 years. Hence, information technological invention, e.g. internet . It will change global economic growth when every person feels need to gather any information from internet or learns any new knowledge from internet as well as any ebook readers only like to read any ebooks. It implies that internet tool can assist many different kinds of industries to grow their business, such as publishing and advertisement industries, ebook publishers, electronic magazine publishers, google, yahoo.com internet advertisement service providers. The internet invention can bring these both industries development because businessmen feel online advertisement is one kind of good advertisement method to help them to promote their businesses to let many clients to know from google or yahoo.com websites as well as

readers had accepted to read ebooks from online in common. It can bring economic growth for these both industries absolutely.

However, in fact, technology has been relatively important in changing financial products and it is necessary to be very precise about what its role has been and will be. AN important form of financial innovation has been the limitation of financial products to sell to different countries, e.g.insurance, share financial products. Internet has also influence many insurance firms or share companies choose to apply online channel to sell any insurance or share financial products to their clients. Hence, internet also influence share investors or insurance buyers' purchase behaviors. They can apply internet to enter the insurance or share firms' websites to choose their preferable insurance plans or share kinds to buy at homes conveniently.

Hence, internet innovation also bring finance industry benefit, it can help it to attract many insurance and share buyers to choose to buy their preferable shares or insurance plans from any insurance firms or share firms very easily. It means that insurance agents or share agents number will be reduce when one day insurance or share buyers begin feel that they do not need any insurance or share agents' helps, then they can gather any insurance or share information to decide whether they ought buy which kind of insurance plans or shares more suitable from internet channel. The unlucky, it will bring the unemployment ratio raises, when general insurance and share buyers feel that they do not need insurance or share agents‘ opinions or they do not believe their opinions. They feel that they can gather any real information concerns any shares or insurance plans to make more accurate judgement more than general insurance or share agents. Then, internet can help insurance or share firms to increase financial products investors number, but it also create unemployment effect to the insurance and share agents.

Most technological change has done something cheaper, faster or with less labor, that is, it has been process innovation rather than product innovation.It can raise productivity, e.g. artificial intelligence , robotic invention, it can help factory workers to manufacture many products, e.g. vehicles, air condition,washing machine etc. machine products in factories in short time. So, robotic can raise efficiency and productivity to any factories nowadays. Anther example of technological change is the electronic processing of cheques, now embodied in CHAPS, clearing house automated payment system. It has been calculated to estimate to same to many bank clerks number would be required in any countries' banks. However, it has not affected the consumer product at all, the method of writing a cheque and time to clear it are the same as in 1889. Similarly, there were large-scale changes in credit card technology in the later 1980s , but these had little effect on the consumer. In many cases in hi-tech products have had little impact, such as EFTPOS, electronic fund transfer at point of sale (who wants to have their bank account debited) at once if they have more weeks‘ free credit with an Access card?. Such any information technological developments may eventually catch no. Such as credit card companies are becoming unhappy with the number of customers who use them to obtain free credit and then pay off the entire balance.

IN consequence, this and the MMC report on credit card (Aug. 1989) will make the use of credit cards less attractive as means of payment and less borrowings. This may make EFTPOS more attractive. So, information technological development also change bank industry service from credit card borrowing service to electronic fund transfer service. It brings the bank saving and borrowing services change to more rapid money transfer and money borrowing service need to bank clients.

Another good illustration of the process / product innovation is on trading exchange. Those dealing in established products, like the international stock
exchange, have introduced electronic dealing. Those dealing in new products use floor trading, for example LIEFE, the London International Financial Futures Exchange. It has been pressures to introduce electronic trading. When many consumers accept to buy any products from website (online shopping). Then, e business or online shopping or ecommerce transaction method will influence consumers' traditional visiting shopping method. Online consumers will attempt to find any products to compare their prices and qualities and functions from photos. Then, they can choose to buy their lastly lovely product from the online merchant website at home rapidly. They only need to pay visa card and register their name and address to the online merchant website for record. Then, their products will be delivered to their homes after one day or more rapidly. So, internet also change general consumers' shopping model or method from visiting shops to online shops. Internet innovation also help any online merchants to raise sale chance in short time when overseas clients can choose their products to buy from internet and they can deliver to their homes.

Thus, the role of technology in process innovation has been crucial and in the product innovation of secondary importance, although some product innovation has been
dependent on technology for example, ATM (cash machine). However, there is an important intermediate category, where technology has reduced the price of something previously feasible to such an extent that it is almost as if it were a new product. Consequently, this may reflect a great availability of such products through technology (supply curve shift) or greater demand for them. It may be purely fashion especially as computerization , e.g. ebooks reading method, e-share or e-insurance plan choice method, can change the most humdrum transaction to influence

readers' reading habit and financial product inventors' investing choice method or investing attitude or reading attitude to every consumers' living attitudes. Hence, information technological innovation will bring large impact to some industries, such as publishing and investing industries in the future.

The nature and causes of unemployment have been controversial issues through out the development of economics. Can information technological development raise unemployment? Any countries' unemployment occurs , it may include different factors, e.g. education factor, low salary factor,skillful workers number shortage factor. More recently, economists have looked at the rate of adjustment of employment (and therefore unemployment) to changes in the real wage rate within the labor market. These wage stickiness models attempt to explain the disequilibrium unemployment which occurs when the real wage is above its equilibrium market clearing rate. So, unemployment in this case is not the caused by adjustment problems in the labor (lacking skill workers supply number) , but results form the optimal behavior, (the real wage is low, so it can not attract many people to seek jobs to do in the labor market).

However, if one day, many jobs or occupations need have high informational technological workers to do. Consequently, it will have many low skill workers lose

jobs because employers won't need low skillful workers , they need high skill workers to do their jobs. For example, auto-machine manufacturing factories will be increased demand if the employers need to manufacture many vehicles in the most efficient speed. They only believe that the high skill workers must apply robotics to help them to manufacture any vehicles to compare low skill workers in short time to achieve raising efficiency and productive vehicles number aim in order to have enough vehicle number to supply to global vehicle clients to choose in short time. So, it means that information technological innovation will influence low skill workers to lose their job absolutely. When some jobs are changed to high skill manufacturing method. Also, it implies that rapid high information technological developed countries will bring high efficiency and productive number effect in possible, but it also bring high unemployment ratio to the low skill workers in possible in the same time.

This consequence will occurs in the same time, it won't occur either high technological development earlier than high unemployment ratio later to workers or high unemployment ratio occurs earlier than high technological development later. Due to high technological development must influence high unemployment ratio to low skill workers. It is the main factor to cause future high unemployment to global high technological product need countries.

Both measures capture the impact of the factors which affect the demand and supply of high technological skill workers. Supply factors alter the size and composition of the workforce who are either in work or looking for work, when demand factors affect the size and composition of the workforce currently employers. So, when the demand and supply of skills need to workers have changed over time. Such as this high technological development need to some countries case, e.g. when China begins to accept high technological development living mode, many Chinese choose to buy any high technological products or many manufacturers need high skillful workers to help them to manufacture any products to achieve the increasing productive number aim in short time efficiently . Consequently, the low skillful Chinese manufacturing workers will lose jobs , if the Chinese manufacturing can choose either employing foreign skillful workers or provide training to the talent workers to learn to achieve their working skillful needs. So, the Chinese low skillful workers will face competition from foreign skillful workers or the high skillful workers. In the result, when China reaches the high information technological development stage, it will have many low skillful workers lose jobs in the same time in possible.It can explain that why the high informational technological development can bring the high unemployment ratio to high skillful workers in the same time.

CHAPTER FOUR

Information technology raises global mobile market competition and economy growth

Nowadays, we will contact different information from different sources, e.g. internet, newspaper, magazine, radio, television. So, our daily lives are influenced by any information and we will analyze the useful information to do any decision, e.g. consumption, entertainment, travelling, learning etc. So, information can influence our societies to develop. However, I believe that , due to internet invention can be applied to mobile invention. Hence, human feel mobile is not only phone call function, it can be applied to link internet to find any data from website in any where and in any time conveniently. I shall indicate some cases to explain how and why internet information can influence mobile to help us to gather any data to do any decisions in any where and any time . So, mobile will bring more influence to our future economy development, I shall explain as below:

As above graphs showed that Ciso (2012) indicated that the mobile traffic is growing rapidly. The mobile IP Traffic had increased 116% from 2006 to 2012 as well as Fixed up traffic had also increased 127% from 1997 to 2003 (Global IP in petabytes per month. So, it seems that future many people will feel need to use mobile to phone call and gather data from internet every day. GSMA intelligence (2014) showed that the total direct and indirect contribution to GDP has 1.9 % contribution to GDP on 2014 for mobile operators as well as related industries had 0.4% contribution to GDP on 2014. Their both GDP share ratio were not too bad to compare general economy and productivity improvement. Hence, any mobile related industry or product will have much needs to global mobile product or related mobile product communication users in the future. US commerce & Forrester (1956 to 2008) and Forrester research (2019 to 2016) showed that the three cycle of technological growth and digestion of industry innovation and growth. Communication equipment GDP ratio had grown up to 1% on 2000. Computer equipment GDP ratio had grown up to 2.5% on 2000. Commercial software GDP ratio had grown up to 3.5% on 2000 year. Although, communication equipment had the least market share ratio , it included the mobile GDP. But on 2000 year, mobile industry is earlier communication invention product. However, the (AI) artificial intelligent mobile products may not been invented to sell in communication market. So, the early mobile can not apply internet to do data gathering tasks for users. It did not very attractive in this period. However, when artificial intelligent mobile is invention, it brings much change to influence many young people feel (AI) mobile is essential communication product and convenience to use in any time and any where. So, the (AI) mobile communication tools will have large market share in the future. Also, its global GDP share ratio will increase rapidly ,because many young people feel mobile is one kind of essential communication product nowadays.

At a time of slowed growth and continued volatility, many countries are looking for policies that will stimulate growth and create new jobs. Information communications technology (ICT) is not only one of the fastest growing industries – directly creating millions of jobs – but it is also an important enabler of innovation and development. The number of mobile subscriptions (6.8 billion) is approaching global population figures, with 40% of people in the world already online. In this new environment, the competitiveness of economies depends on their ability to leverage new technologies. The information technology can bring these common economic effects of ICT.

1. Direct job creation

The ICT sector is, and is expected to remain, one of the largest employers. In the US alone, computer and information technology jobs are expected to grow by 22% up to 2020, creating 758,800 new jobs. In Australia, building and running the new super-fast National Broadband Network will support 25,000 jobs annually. Naturally, the growth in different segments is uneven. In the US, for each job in the high-tech industry, five additional jobs, on average, are created in other sectors. In

2013, the global tech market will grow by 8%, creating jobs, salaries and a widening range of services and products.

2. Contribution to GDP growth

Findings from various countries confirm the positive effect of ICT on growth. For example, a 10% increase in broadband penetration is associated with a 1.4% increase in GDP growth in emerging markets. In China, this number can reach 2.5%. The doubling of mobile data use caused by the increase in 3G connections boosts GDP per capita growth rate by 0.5% globally. The Internet accounts for 3.4% of overall GDP in some economies. Most of this effect is driven by e-commerce – people advertising and selling goods online.

3. Emergence of new services and industries

Numerous public services have become available online and through mobile phones. The transition to cloud computing is one of the key trends for modernization. The government of Moldova is one of the first countries in Eastern Europe and Central Asia to shift its government IT infrastructure into the cloud and launch mobile and e-services for citizens and businesses. ICT has enabled the emergence of a completely new sector: the app industry. Research shows that Facebook apps alone created over 182,000 jobs in 2011, and that the aggregate value of the Facebook app economy exceeds $$12 billion.

4. Workforce transformation

Information technology is developed by companies like oDesk, Amazon and Samasource, help to divide tasks into small components that can then be outsourced to contract workers. The contractors are often based in emerging economies. Microwork platforms allow entrepreneurs to significantly cut costs and get access to qualified workers. In 2012, oDesk alone had over 3 million registered contractors who performed 1.5 million tasks. This trend had spillover effects on other industries, such as online payment systems. ICT has also contributed to the rise of entrepreneurship, making it much easier for self-starters to access best practices, legal and regulatory information, marketing and investment resources.

5. Business innovation

In OECD countries, more than 95% of businesses have an online presence. The Internet provides them with new ways of reaching out to customers and competing for market share. Over the past few years, social media has established itself as a powerful marketing tool. ICT tools employed within companies help to streamline business processes and improve efficiency. The unprecedented explosion of connected devices throughout the world has created new ways for businesses to serve their customers.

● How the Smartphone has Impacted Economic Development

The evolution of the smartphone saw communication equipment that was designed for business use quickly transform into smaller and smaller consumer devices. The BlackBerry was the desired phone for busy executives, and then in 2007 Apple introduced the first iPhone. These phones, and the many apps that soon followed, changed the way we communicate, do business, entertain ourselves, socially interact with others, and learn. Technology has long been a driver of economic development throughout the world, but it is only recently that mobile technology – and smartphones in particular – have been significant economic factors. One reason is that much of the manufacturing of the phones themselves is performed overseas.

According to a major report conducted by GSMA, the mobile economy contributed an estimated $2.4 trillion to the international economy in 2013, representing about 3.6% of global gross domestic product. This number includes more than 10 million jobs created, and contributed at least $336 billion to public funding in the United States alone. Not only that, but the size of the mobile economy is growing at an aggressive pace, with estimates that it could contribute as much as 5.1% to global GDP by 2020.

● How Smartphones Relate to the Mobile Economy

One of the clearest indications that smartphones are an integral part of the mobile economy, and the economy at large, is the fact that so many people now have them. According to the Pew Research Center, an estimated 64% of adults in the United States own a smartphone, while 90% of American adults own a cell phone of some kind. As smartphones continue to drop in price and increase in functionality, that 64% will inevitably increase.

Globally, smartphone penetration has almost doubled in the past five years. In 2010, it was estimated that about 20% of the global population used smartphones, while by 2014 that number was estimated at 37%. If we look as far back as 2008 – which is the first full year that Apple's iPhone was available (and is widely regarded to herald the start of the modern smartphone era) – that number has more than tripled, from about 12% in 2008 to the 37% we see in 2014.

● Economic Impact of Smartphones and Apps

There are numerous business articles that conclude smartphones have contributed to economic globalization and growth as they've been adopted at arguably unprecedented rates. The following are a few ways in which smartphones have contributed to economic development around the world.

There is no question that the ability to communicate with others from anywhere in the world has contributed significantly to economic growth. However, it has also helped companies save money on expenses that are simply no longer necessary. For example, mobile-compatible conferencing software, such as Citrix's GoToMeeting, allows smartphone users to share both voice and data from worksites or any other mobile location. This reduces delays and substantially decreases the need for executives to physically travel to locations around the world.

- Creation of a Brand-New "App Economy"

The creation of the "app economy" has also been a major boom for the economy at large. In fact, even as early as 2012, it was estimated that there were around 500,000 jobs created as a result of the app economy. It is worth noting that the estimate does not include the design, manufacture, or marketing of smartphones and other mobile devices.

- Lower Barriers to Entry

One of the other benefits of the so-called app economy is the dramatically lower barrier to entry that this new sector offers. Instead of requiring a massive manufacturing capacity or labor pool, entrepreneurial individuals can take a great idea, learn how or hire someone to code, and utilize the platforms built by Apple, Google, or Microsoft to distribute their software solution to a truly global market.

- Ability to Better Utilize Excess Capacity

One of the other major advances that smartphones have facilitated via the app economy is the growth of apps that utilize "excess capacity." Excess capacity is an economic term that refers to capital or other assets that are being underutilized.

Perhaps the best example of this is Uber, the ridesharing app that is taking the world by storm and severely disrupting the taxi industry. Uber allows anyone with a car, presuming the car is new enough and well maintained, to use it to get paid for giving other people rides. Uber, through the use of their smartphone app, is able to manage drivers with riders very effectively, reducing costs associated with getting a ride. Car owners are able to utilize their vehicles that would otherwise just sit idle.

● How mobile information technological product brings economic impact on the Developing World

Another incredible impact of the smartphone is its ability to bridge the technology and infrastructure gap that exists in the developing world. Cellular signal is far more practical than hardwiring telephone and data lines in many parts of the developing world. Access to mobile technology, and increasingly affordable smartphones, offers incredible promise and economic opportunities for companies across the globe.

While moonshot projects like Google's Project Loon are at the very least they offer a long-term trend in the developing world, including greater access around the world to the global economy, facilitated by the increasingly ubiquitous smartphone. As we continue to improve their functionality and ease of use, smartphones will remain an essential part of the economy.

● How is the mobile economy changing the global economy?

We now live in a world shaped and defined by our ability to reach friends, loved ones, business partners and the legions of people in our networks no matter where we are and no matter how far away they may be. And we don't just reach into our pockets and pull out a device that lets us talk with one another. We video-chat, we share photos, we transmit biomedical data, we access all manner of written and high-definition video media, we work and we play in more ways than probably anyone could now quantify. Our children will never know a world when this wasn't possible, yet a decade and a half ago these wireless wonders science fiction. Now, the mobile technology behind this age of connectivity isn't just enhancing and defining our daily lives, it is guiding and enriching our communities and our world on a macroeconomic level. How the mobile industry, it just keeps growing.

A new study from the Boston Consulting Group sought to analyse the economic impact of mobile communications on consumers, businesses and nations, with deeper examinations of the impact on Brazil, China, Germany, India, South Korea and the United States. The results, drawn from government, engineering and market data, as well as surveys of businesses and consumers, are eye-opening, especially for the users of wireless technology.

The expanding 4G networks , even future 5G networks that are already widespread in many industrialized nations offer data speeds that are 12,000 times faster than the speeds of 2G or 3G networks speed, one of the most resonating engineering miracles in history.

At the same time, mobile subscription costs per megabyte of transmitted data fell 99% from 2005 to 2013, and smartphones are now available for as little as $40. The reason mobility is so affordable: scale. In less than 15 years, adoption of 3G and 4G technology has grown to nearly 3 billion connections, and that number is expected to exceed 8 billion by 2020.Even future 5G technology will bring (AI) mobiles to be more attractive to persuade communication consumers to continue to feel need to buy to use.

Meanwhile, in the six countries surveyed, the annual value of mobile gross domestic product, or mGDP – spending on mobile devices, mobile connectivity and mobile commerce – is more than $1.2 trillion. Yes, trillion. The United States has the largest absolute mGDP, standing at $548 billion, or about 3.2% of GDP, which exceeds the economic contribution of the auto industry. The Boston Consulting Group also calculated the aggregate value of mobile technologies – the value derived by consumers from use of their wireless devices – to be roughly $6.4 trillion. Moreover, mobile technology is especially valuable for consumers in emerging markets. BCG reports that in China and India, the value to consumers exceeded 40% of their annual income.

- Why will (AI) mobile tool be continue to use in popular in communication market.

In the future, (AI) mobile does not only to be accepted to use for homeholder individual or family , it can be accepted to feel to need to use for businesses, even it can create more new jobs. It also levels the playing field for small and medium-sized enterprises, the report found. SMEs that reported using at least three mobile applications in their operations or marketing and sales work saw revenue rise two times faster than other similarly sized firms and created jobs up to six times faster than their peers. In emerging markets, mobile tech is allowing SMEs to leapfrog older generations of technology still widely used in more industrialized countries, and the percentage of these “mobile leaders” in China, India and Brazil is higher than in their more developed counterparts.

The study predicts that if more SMEs expanded at the rate of the “mobile leaders”, an additional 7 million jobs could be created in the six countries studied over the next three years.

The study finds a direct correlation between these technological advances and their economic benefits, and the rule-of-law systems that allows this innovation to take place and be brought to market. It notes the core technology innovators for 2G, 3G and 4G , even future 5G network wireless – Qualcomm is among them – “take enormous risks by spending heavily on research and development with no guarantee of return on investment. Companies focused on mobile’s core technologies invest a larger share of revenue (21%) in R&D than any other industry except biotechnology – and more than all other R&D-heavy industries.” And that, the study concludes, offers a roadmap for future development technologically and economically.

The vast majority of surveyed consumers, they want faster data speeds, more wireless coverage, more battery life and many other improvements – at a time when data traffic is already expected to increase by 1,000 times before this decade is over. Such future growth, BCG says, depends on continuing the policies that enabled the growth to date, including “strong patent protection to encourage large and risky investments in mobile technology innovation”, and preservation of the wireless industry standards process that brings together companies from throughout the industry to solve complex technology problems and make those solutions widely shared.

This extraordinary change isn’t ancient history. We have seen the wondrous pace of technological evolution accelerate before our eyes, and we know why it happened and what it has accomplished. At a time when regulators and legislators are reexamining patent laws and pondering the best ways to nurture innovation, it is worth policy-makers and industry leaders taking a moment to look at this mobile evolution, this mobile revolution, and think about what we must do to keep these advances going.

● Big Data’s Economic Impact to raise (AI) mobile need.

Big Data is beginning to have a significant impact on our knowledge of the world. This is important because increases in human knowledge have always played a large role in increasing economic activity and living standards. Continued improvements in the price and capacity of tools for collecting, transmitting, storing, analyzing and acting upon data will make it easier to gather more information and to turn it into actionable knowledge of how systems work.

Big Data is best understood as an untapped resource that technology finally allows us to exploit. For instance, data on weather, insects, and crop plantings has always existed. But it is now possible to cost-effectively collect those data and use them in an informed manner. We can keep a record of every plant's history, including sprayings and rainfall. When we drive a combine over the field, equipment can identify every plant as either crop or weed and selectively apply herbicide to just the weeds. It is one good example to be used on agricultural industry aspect. So, farmers can earn more benefits when they apply big data to gather any weather, insects and crop plantings information to decide when is the suitable time to grow crop on farm any time when they touch their (AI) mobile tool in any time and anywhere very conveniently.

Such new use of data has the capacity to transform every industry in similar ways. A recent OECD report listed some of the ways that more and better data will affect the economy, they may include as below:

Producing new goods and services, such as the Nest home thermometer or mass customized shoes; Optimizing business processes; More-targeted marketing that injects customer feedback into product design; Better organizational management; and faster innovation through a shorter research and development cycle.

A report from McKinsey Global Institute estimates that Big Data could generate an additional $3 trillion in value every year in just seven industries. Of this, $1.3 trillion would benefit the United States. The report also estimated that over half of this value would go to customers in forms such as fewer traffic jams, easier price comparisons, and better matching between educational institutions and students. Note that some of these benefits do not affect GDP or personal income as we measure them. They do, however, imply a better quality of life.

The impact affects more than consumers, however. Erik Brynjolfsson of MIT found that companies that adopt data-driven decision making achieve 5 to 6 percent higher productivity and output growth than their peers, even after controlling for other investments and the use of information technology. Similar differences were found in asset utilization, return on equity, and market value.

Moreover, the Omidyar Network recently released a study of the impact of Open Data policies on government. The report concluded that implementation of these policies could boost annual income within the G20 by between $700 billion and $950 billion. The benefits include reduced corruption, better workplace conditions, increased energy efficiency, and improved foreign trade.

Even the advertising industry, whose use of data is sometimes viewed with suspicion, delivers large benefits. A study by the Direct Marketers

Association found that better use of data made marketing more efficient both by allowing companies to avoid sending solicitations to individuals who are unlikely to buy their product and by matching customers with offers that better meet their individual needs and interests. Big data also reduced barriers to entry by making it easier for small companies to get useful market data. Finally, another McKinsey study concluded that free Internet services underwritten by Internet advertising delivered significant benefits to Internet users. It estimated the social surplus from these services at 120 billion euros, 80 percent of which went to consumers.

This trend in data also has an impact on workers. Data analysis has been called "the sexiest job of the 21st century." The United States already has an estimated 500,000 Big Data jobs. But McKinsey estimates that there is a shortage of between 140,000 and 190,000 workers with advanced degrees in statistics, computer engineering and other applied fields. Perhaps more important is the shortage of 1.5 million managers and analysts who hold traditional jobs but are capable of integrating Big Data into their decision making. The need to understand and act on improved data is likely to increase worker productivity and pay.

When scientists continued to invent any technological improvements, data will become even easier to collect, transmit, store, and analyze. Together with related advances in material sciences, biotechnology, information technology, and nanotechnology, it will enable a vast range of new products and services. As with any resource, the main constraint will be the ability to imagine new uses for this resource and to build a viable business model around these uses that delivers valuable products and services to consumers.

● Future mobile data usage and traffic growth

In 2022, monthly mobile data traffic per active smartphone in North America will reach 25 GB . Smartphones have become an inseparable part of our daily lives. Waking up with a morning alarm, using Whatsapp, listening to music, reading News, watching YouTube videos, checking emails, updating project status and so on, everything is seamlessly executed from mobile apps installed on our mobile devices. Currently, 2.1 Billion people worldwide own a Smartphone and according to TouchPoints report. It indicated that adults aged 25 plus use their phone about 264 times a day, including texts and calling . For people aged 15-24, the number is 387 times every day. If average sleeping time for this age group is taken 10 hours, this

equates to some sort of Smartphone activity every other minute.
This is unbelievable yet true. Hence, the use of Smartphone and mobile applications are not going to get reduced in 2019 anyways. Only mobile app trends might show new colors. In this blog post, we are going to discuss the current mobile app development trends that you are going to look in 2019.

- Future mobile App Development Trends

Accelerated Mobile Pages (AMP) Is Changing Web App Landscape: It's been 3 years since Google has started the AMP Project. Apart from that, Google also announced that there will be a separate search index for the mobile web. This revolutionary step changed the mobile app development trends completely especially from SEO and Web app perspective.
AI scientists found, there will be a more than 300% increase in investment on artificial intelligence next year compared to 2018. Through the use of advanced analytics, cognitive interfaces into complex systems, and machine learning techs, AI will provide business users access to powerful insights never before available to them. Due to these advantages, big bees like Google, IBM, eBay, Facebook have started acquiring startups those who are adept in Artificial Intelligence and machine learning.

- Cloud-Driven Mobile Apps Are Rising

From customers to tech professionals, everyone has heard about cloud technology and how it's impacting our collective lives. Today, cloud computing has finally found it's place with mobile apps. Now, we can expect powerful mobile apps which directly fetch data from the cloud and take minimum space in your smartphone internal memory. Google Drive, Dropbox, & OneDrive are only the tip of the iceberg. A Cisco research says– Globally, cloud apps will drive 90% of total mobile data traffic by the end of 2019, and Mobile cloud traffic will be 11-fold with compound annual growth rate (CAGR) of 60%.

The Prime goal of an enterprise mobile app is to help you restructure, streamline and manage crucial business processes on the go. Whereas, A micro-app aims to suffice very targeted operations and takes less load. However, both are successfully accomplishing their endeavors and are expected to continue further. An example of enterprise mobile apps can be the Evernote through which your teams can collaborate on projects from their mobile devices. On the other hand, Facebook messenger or to-do list app are good examples of micro-apps that concentrates on only one task.

An Adobe study says 77% of business owners found enterprise apps advantageous & 66% are increasing their investment further. Also, the 430 billion enterprise app market is expected by 2021. Moreover, micro-apps with features like lightweight, targeted, HTML & ad-hoc based, are rising these days. Hence, these mobile app development trends are expected to stay constant in 2019.

Innovative Healthcare application development technologies point to better care that will expand care beyond traditional methods. These devices show that it's way beyond getting restricted to the only the healthcare industry and prove to be one of the promising mobile app development trends in 2019.

● M-Commerce Is Becoming A New Standard

These days, instead of using Credit/Debit cards, a considerable number of customers is preferring to make purchases through Google Pay and Apple Pay. This is giving a push to m-commerce. Coupled with wearable devices with m-commerce payment facility will take a different shape in 2019. Beyond predictive analytics and data collection, the wearable market will also play a major role in the future of M-commerce and customer loyalty.

It is a market prediction from these mobile app development trends. So, internet of Things will Be much need.

The rapid adoption of cloud-based apps brings us to one of the latest mobile app development trends that have piqued mobile developer interest in 2019 – the Internet of Things or IoT. A per reports from IDC, spending on IoT is expected to reach up to $745 billion this year, and surpass $22 Billion by 2022! This directly impacts the mobile app trends as IoT devices are majorly controlled by Smartphones. Here's the predicted growth curve of IoT-

Beacons & Location Based Services Are on the rise. Integrated location-based service applications like Apple's iBeacons and Google Beacon are popular. Wi-Fi usage will no longer be limited to hotels, restaurants, retail outlets and in health-care. The usage of applications with Wi-Fi support is going to rise beyond these traditional requirements will help people with relevant location-based information. So, cloud -based apps will assist mobiles communication tools to apply on hotel, restaurant, cinema etc. entertainment service industries in the future.

● Technology And Its Impact On Consumer Behavior

Often a company leadership faces challenges especially when it comes to the rapid technological changes. Since the emergence of information technology, company communication with its customers took a turn to an unknown destination. Just think back ten years ago or even 5 years, how were businesses reaching their customers? How were customers reaching them? Compare that to how communication is passing between the two parties now and who is driving it. Technology has placed the power in the customers' hands literally with the internet enabled smart phone and tablets. Note, that these devices are always being improved such that the newest version offers more to the consumers, making the previous one obsolete in as little as six months' time.

How and why has technology changed the way consumers behave? Customers are connected to apply technology to achieve any service transaction easily , e.g. mobile communication tool. Almost everybody is living two lives, an online life and a somewhat boring offline one. We are all connected in one platform or another through our network of friends. We also own more than one device that keeps us updated. This means that we thrive on being active and informed online, and Exact Target Marketing content verified this from a study they did, whereby 91% of consumers indicated that access to content across all devices was important.

Information technology advancements fuel the connectivity that brings together the world as one big community, from the smart phones to super-fast data. This trend is not about to change because now kids as young as 5 years know how to operate a smart phone, LinkedIn even lowered its age limit to 13years to capitalize on the technology adoption rate. Companies need to meet the consumers where they are and satisfy their sophisticated needs. If your target market spends more time on Instagram or Twitter, be present and respond to them on the same platform. Are you doing enough to leverage technology and handle the informed consumer?

- Why do consumer expectations have changed ?

In the past, as a company you set the times that you were open for business, and customers had to put up with it or stay without that particular product. Technology has totally changed that, with the introduction of e-commerce and mobile phones, customers can access products at anytime. They have raised expectations on what is acceptable customer service and what is not. As a business, you have to keep up with the changed consumer behavior or be out of business. For example, if a customer wants to purchase something online at night and has a query, they expect to get instant answers. If they do not they choose another supplier from the myriad available online who can meet their immediate need. Consumers now understand the power they have and will use it when not satisfied with a service. A simple expression of their dissatisfaction on your social media that is not responded to immediately will ignite uproar from other customers who were accepted with your products and service.

● Smart phone will be future new communication channels

In the past, a company provided customer service through emails –that did not get prompt responses – and phone calls. These two communication tools had their own challenges and favored the company more; it was at their discretion what information to give out.

This age however, is very refreshed. Social media platforms and live chat place you right in front of your customer; you cannot sacrifice your customer to maintain your brand position. Actually, when you do not respond to a query, you damage your brand reputation because that information is accessible to millions of people.These new tools is that you have a wider data collection pool; you can fast track your research and development by utilizing the big data.

In conclusion, we have seen the growth of technology and its impact on consumer behavior. We have looked at three ways that consumer behavior has changed, from connected consumers to changed expectations and new communication tools use. I believe the statement "Customer is King" has never been experienced by companies like in this information technology. Customers now know they are powerful, what are you doing to quench their instant information thirst.

● The growing importance of the smart mobile technology economy

Technology has deeply affected the global economy and its usage has been linked to marketplace transformation, improved living standards and more robust international trade. So, if technology has virtually revolutionized every industry in the current global economy, why economists still question whether technology is visible in traditional economic metrics such as GDP, productivity, and corporate profits?

Technological advances have significantly improved operations and lowered the cost of doing business. Currently, as an example, just a few technicians controlling robotic systems can operate an entire manufacturing plant, and innovative inventory systems are capable of supplying needed parts within a short time for assembly. Advancements in the computer industry, coupled with advancements in telecommunications, have increased job opportunities and strengthened economic growth.

All physical barriers to communication over distances have been properly overcome by the internet. In a similar way, manufacturing and consumer goods companies have developed online links to their suppliers and customer support. Suppliers can keep track of production line efficiencies through automated systems and can more efficiently ship parts and materials to the required locations, reducing inventory and downtime. In addition to that ecommerce and online banking capabilities have also helped reduce the cost of doing business. Within this new context, and given the fast-paced emergence of disruptive products and business models, as well as the transformative power of digital technologies on business and society, executives must become masters of the global "technology economy", being capable of detecting the economic impact of such fast technological changes and respond with similar speed and foresight.

Many researches from many respected companies, such as BCG, IMF and World Economic Forum show that whenever companies cut back on technology investments aiming to shore up profits, the result is the opposite, as profits sink significantly, and, as a side effect, GDP also falls dramatically, then a chain reaction starts with the fall of labor productivity after a few years.

As a matter of fact, what companies are really doing is cutting back on an important investment that could create the next growth wave and, in many instances, that investment could generate huge leverage, helping to lower costs and expenses much faster than technology spending rises, but companies can only achieve that by managing their technology spending properly. To do that, senior executives require new metrics and new ways of thinking. In order to successfully navigate the technology economics scenario and leverage optimum business performance, executives must create, measure, and track virtual economic measures just as carefully as they follow metrics about the physical world.

- How smart mobile brings the impact of technology economy

The impact of technology economy in the market is very significant, infusing even the measurement of the market economy. Some of the largest indexes known in the market, such as the Dow Jones Industrial Average (DJIA) and the S&P 500, have changed. Tech powerhouses like Apple,

Google, and Amazon, whose stocks are valued much higher than those of many long-time industrial members, are replacing large industrial super companies. Apple, with its high market capitalization, accounts for such a large share of the DJIA, for example, that any hiccup in its quarterly earnings can move the entire index, situation that was once done by other large corporations such as GM and Caterpillar.

● More on digital transformation:

Technology has an amazing power of permeate companies. An important measurement of the technology economy is the observing the Worldwide IT Spending volume, which is regarding the corporate spending for hardware, software, data centers, networks, and staff, both internal and outsourced IT services. Currently, this volume is close to USD6 trillion per year. To put this number on a more illustrative perspective, if we were to consider the global technology economy a country and its yearly spending its GDP, it would be ranked as the world's third largest economy, between the economies of China and Japan and more than twice the size of the UK economy.

Technology spending, gross margins and economic growth have a strong relationship when measured by productivity and GDP. A good example is that executives can predict with some accuracy the impact on the overall economy of a decline in technology spending. Whenever companies cut back on discretionary spending in order to improve profits during a downturn, they slash their investments in technology. Soon afterward, GDP falls dramatically, and, within a few years, labor productivity across the economy falls, as technological innovation is an important component of productivity. The drop in technology intensity that results from a decline in technology spending causes the labor force to decrease, which shows up in productivity up to three years later because productivity is a "stickier" measure.

As a matter of fact, whenever considering a company's productivity, it possible to observe not only a connection between technology intensity and gross margins but also a strong correlation, which means that technology intensity and gross margins tend to rise and decline together, one as a consequence of the other. It's possible to set as a recent example of this effect before and after the recent world economic crash that started in 2007, when companies were investing more and more heavily in technology relative to revenues and operating expenses, and gross margins were rising.

That trend accelerated through 2008 and until 2009, when companies realized what had happened and began to cut technology investment dramatically. After that, technology intensity dropped precipitously along with gross margins.

Within most companies around the globe, in every single industry, technology investment is growing faster than revenues and, in many cases, faster than the GDP of any country. It is clear to all companies that technology is vital to to the successful operations of companies and, mainly, to the global economy, but being able to manage technology spending properly within a few years ahead will require an increasingly sophisticated way of looking at the world and at a company's performance.

With that in mind, it is essential for companies to control, adapt, and optimize investments in real-time according to market conditions and on the basis of new forms of market data. Companies need to consider all inputs and outcomes and look at technology economically to gain competitive advantage before competitors do. Finally, if executives understand it and look at technology investments this way, it will not only matter, it will make all the difference for the their companies and for the global economy.

● Why and how can smart mobile information technology encourage the growth of global mobile economy ?

Has smart phone communication technology bring a small device ever had a bigger impact? Around the world, the smartphone, along with its cousin, the tablet, and a fast-expanding family of "wearables" and other "smart" devices are transforming the way people live, work, play, connect, and interact. In the process, they are converting the digital revolution into an increasingly mobile phenomenon.

Consumers put a value on the mobile Internet that far exceeds what they pay for it. Competition and innovation in the tech sector are unleashing invention in countless other areas as consumers adopt new behavior patterns and businesses find ways to improve efficiency, develop new products and services, and expand their market reach. The mobile Internet has created millions of jobs, too. Mobile penetration is increasing, the costs of access and devices are coming down, and more and more people in both developed and developing economies are using the mobile Internet as their first—and often their only—means of going online.

To be sure, there remain big issues of infrastructure, remote-area access, privacy, and data security, among others, to be addressed. But the combination of consumer demand and market-based innovation has consistently and successfully driven the mobile Internet's growth, generating enormous economic and social benefits. As we have argued before, for almost everyone on the planet today, regardless of where he or she lives and works, the mobile Internet is already, or soon will be, a life-changing phenomenon. (See Through the Mobile Looking Glass: The Transformative Potential of Mobile Technologies, BCG Focus, April 2013.)

(The first report examined the mobile Internet's economic impact in the EU5; see The Mobile Internet Economy in Europe, BCG report, December 2014.) It provides an overview of the reach, ramifications, and potential of the mobile Internet so that policy makers and other leaders can better assess its current and future impact and pursue policies that foster its continued growth.

How can explode Demand for Mobile Access and Services ? The numbers tell one part of the story. There are currently almost 7 billion mobile phone subscriptions globally, or one for every person on Earth. More than a third of these are smartphone subscriptions. Global smartphone sales are expected to have grown 18 percent in 2014, led by big emerging markets such as China, India, and Indonesia, as average unit prices fall. Mobile Internet penetration worldwide has doubled from 18 percent in 2011 to 36 percent today; by 2017, mobile access will exceed fixed-line access, with 54 percent penetration compared with 51 percent. At that point, mobile will account for almost 60 percent of all spending on Internet access.

Several factors are fuelling this growth, including expanding coverage, increasingly sophisticated mobile-device functionality, sharply falling prices and fast-rising sales, a growing selection of smartphones and tablets on the market, and the development of new categories of devices such as wearables and connected home devices. Another factor is more reliable data connections that enable increasingly data-intensive activities. Some 60 percent of the world's population is now covered by 3G connectivity. The EU has 90 percent 3G coverage. The U.S. has 96 percent 4G coverage. Even Mount Everest is online—with 4G connectivity at 17,000 feet. Wi-Fi hot spots proliferate as well. In developing markets where 3G and Wi-Fi coverage is sparser, developers are optimizing apps to reach consumers on older 2G networks. One example is Nanu, a free-call app that operates like Skype or Viber but is optimized for 2G networks. Hence, the 5G network communication need users will increase, when they need rapid speed to gather any data.

While much has been written on the infrastructure and related challenges facing mobile technologies, consumer demand remains strong. (See "Delivering Digital Infrastructure," BCG article, April 2014.) This article indicated that the volume of mobile Internet data traffic will continue to expand, driven primarily by increased demand for streaming of video and music content on mobile Internet devices. Global demand for such services will drive up data traffic sevenfold by 2017, from 1.2 terabytes per month in 2013, supported by more 4G networks coming online and existing operators increasing their speed, coverage, and capacity.

● The Launch of Apple and Android Devices Triggered an Explosion in Global Mobile Data Traffic - Connected World: Growth of the Global Mobile Internet Economy

As the mobile revolution has gathered steam, intensifying competition in operating systems and technology has led to fast-paced innovation in smart-device functionality. Nokia and Ericsson launched the first smart devices with multimedia features in 2000. BlackBerry contributed major advances with such innovations as push e-mail and encryption between 2001 and 2007. The launch of Apple's iOS and Google's Android operating systems led to a step change in the user experience with the widespread adoption of the touch screen and easy-to-use, full-featured mobile Web browsing and the rapid rise of third-party-app ecosystems.

Competition among operating systems and their app ecosystems has also triggered an explosion in device development and sales, as well as in global mobile data traffic. In many markets, especially in the developed world, smartphones have rapidly come to dominate mobile phone sales as competition provides consumers and businesses alike with more choice, cheaper devices, and new products. Average smartphone selling prices fell 25 percent worldwide between 2011 and 2013 and are expected to drop a further 19 percent by 2017, for reasons that include falling manufacturing and development costs, market saturation in some developed economies, and prolonged upgrade cycles.

● Smartphone Selling Prices Are Expected to Continue Falling - Connected

World: Growth of the Global Mobile Internet Economy

Choices for consumers abound. There are more than 18,000 Android mobile-device models currently in circulation, manufactured by a host of third-party OEMs. Global tablet sales will have surpassed 260 million units in 2014; according to the Pew Research Center, 42 percent of Americans 18 years and older own a tablet. TVs are increasingly becoming connected devices that can run apps and perform computing functions as well as display broadcast programming. Wearables—smart watches, connected glasses, and fitness monitors (so far)—are a new product category, and market growth and size projections vary. IDC predicts that total wearable shipments will grow from 19 million units in 2014 to 128 million in 2018. Connected technology is being built into more and more automobiles, homes, and machines. Estimates put the ultimate number of connected devices in the Internet of Things—machines or devices that communicate directly with other machines or devices—at around 30 billion.

- Internet and smart phone bring a revolution in communication Behavior

From shopping to sharing to socializing, the mobile experience is a whole new universe of connectivity that's local (it's always where you are), personal (tailored to your needs and preferences), social (all your friends are there as well)—and it's always on. Continuous access to information, communication, friends, and entertainment—among myriad other things—is changing the way billions of people go about their daily lives. Sharing photos and videos on the move is now commonplace, as are tweeting, pinning, and posting. Of Facebook's 829 million active daily users in June 2014, 654 million (almost 80 percent) were mobile users. Much has been made of the role of smartphones in social uprisings and the response to natural disasters. We regularly watch images on the evening news shot not on professional video cameras but on smartphones.

Travelers today use their phones to board planes, unlock hotel rooms, monitor devices at home (temperature and alarm settings, for example), and check in via live video with their families. Mobile payments are common in many economies; mobile apps are transforming banking. The lines between traditional retail, e-commerce, and m-commerce have blurred almost to the point of distinction in some markets, as consumers research online, offline, and on the go and buy wherever and however they find the best selection, service, and deals. Moreover, customized mobile technologies and apps provide services to countless sub segments of consumers with highly particular needs.

Consumers realize an enormous benefit from all this activity, which can be quantified using an economic concept called consumer surplus—that is, the perceived value that consumers themselves believe they receive, over and above what they pay for devices, apps, services, and access. The mobile Internet's total consumer surplus across the 13 countries in our sample is about $3.5 trillion a year, or about $4,000 per individual user. In the developed countries surveyed, the per capita surplus is $5,600, while in the sample's developing markets it averages $2,250.Consumer surplus and the other benefits of the mobile Internet are only set to grow—potentially exponentially. An entire generation of 18- to 34-year-olds, a larger group than the baby boomers, already accesses the Internet primarily through their mobile devices. A 2014 Nielsen survey in the U.S. found that more than 85 percent of these people own a smartphone. Young people in the 18- to 24-year-old age bracket spend an average of 37 hours and 6 minutes per month—the equivalent of almost a full working week—using their phones. Another survey found that almost 20 percent of U.S. Millennials use only their smart devices to go online.

Hence, the mobile Internet is creating entirely new businesses and business models, as well as transforming traditional companies. All kinds of businesses are using mobile technologies to improve operations, cut costs, and reach new markets and customers. The digital economy is flourishing on mobile devices as consumers access and buy apps, music, videos, books, magazines, and other content anytime from anywhere and receive many purchases instantly. They can also buy physical goods on the go using dedicated retailer apps from brick-and-mortar stores such as Walmart, Belle International, and Crom? or from online shopping platforms such as Amazon, Rakuten, and Taobao.

The app economy is flourishing. There have been more than 200 billion cumulative downloads of mobile apps from the various app stores since 2008. The rate of growth is mind-boggling: more than 100 billion downloads took place in 2013 alone. The app economy already contributes $26 billion to GDP and has created some 800,000 jobs in the 13 countries in our sample. For example, payment apps are increasingly popular, and some businesses are cutting out the cash register altogether (DASH, GoCardless, Uber, and Hailo, for example.) There are more mobile bank accounts in Kenya than in

Kansas, but banks in the U.S. and other developed markets are using mobile apps to transform the banking experience for consumers (you can deposit a check by taking a picture)—and are winning plaudits from their customers in the process.

Retailers are embracing m-commerce. With 10 percent of mobile purchases from Wal-mart now happening at stores, CEO Doug McMillon told the 2014 Code Conference that his company is moving to "geo-fence" and "price-promote" store by store—essentially turning each of the company's 11,000 stores into its own multichannel shopping environment with its own product and price promotions. According to Walmart, customers viewed more than 1.5 billion pages on its site during the five days between Thanksgiving and Cyber Monday in November 2014, with about 70 percent of this traffic coming from mobile devices. The Subway restaurant chain uses geo targeting technology to send notifications of personalized deals to Subcard owners' phones when these customers are near a store. France's Groupe Casino employs near-field communication (NFC) tags on shelves to help visually impaired customers download product information to their phones. It also uses NFC technology to help all customers track costs and speed up checkout. Some reports showed that some 60 percent of global mobile consumers use mobile devices as their primary or exclusive means of going online, and more than 80 percent of these people say they will make a purchase on a mobile device in the next 12 months, according to InMobi, a mobile advertising company. Forrester Research expects that m-commerce sales will have made up 29 percent of U.S. consumers' online purchases in 2014, up from 21 percent the previous year. Our research shows m-commerce in the U.S. jumping 60 percent, from $72 billion in 2013 to $115 billion in 2014, and continuing to rise to $245 billion in 2017. Projected growth rates in developing markets are even more dramatic. In India, m-commerce will grow from $6 billion in 2013 to more than $14 billion in 2017. M-commerce in Brazil is projected to have grown 96 percent 2014 and will exceed $5 billion by 2017. In China, m-commerce will grow from $30 billion in 2013 to more than $160 billion by 2017. On November 11, 2014—Singles' Day, China's biggest shopping day of the year—mobile shopping sites handled 1 billion yuan ($163 million) in transactions in the first hour. Total merchandise sales volume settled through Alipay (Alibaba's e-payment affiliate) was approximately $4 billion (24.3 yuan), or 43 percent of all merchandise volume—double the 21 percent volume in 2013.

It's not just a retail phenomenon, either. All kinds of businesses are finding innovative ways to put mobile devices and technologies to work. According to one survey in the U.S., more than 85 percent of B2B customers access content on their mobile devices. Another survey found that at least 50 percent read reviews, access product information, and compare features using mobile devices. While m-commerce currently accounts for only 3 to 5 percent of B2B sales, these numbers are bound to grow as more users apply the lessons of the B2C marketplace to their businesses. IDC calculates that 14 percent of all tablet shipments in 2014 (which it estimates at about 245 million) went to commercial organizations, up from 11 percent in 2013. It expects the percentage of commercial shipments to increase to 18 percent by 2018.

● Developing Economies Embrace the Mobile Internet to China and India high population countries

Access to the mobile Internet continues to grow quickly around the world, especially in developing markets, where limited fixed-line access and the relative ease of deploying mobile networks make the mobile Internet particularly well suited. In China, for example, there were 632 million Internet users as of the middle of 2014, or about 45 percent of the total population. In sub-Saharan Africa, mobile penetration is about 60 percent, compared with less than 2 percent for fixed-line access. Ultimately, entire nations in Africa will access the Internet only through mobile devices.

As mobile infrastructure is built and mobile usage increases, consumers benefit from the new services that grow up around these devices. The number of Chinese consumers using mobile devices to buy goods jumped 42 percent to 205 million in 2014. Facebook has 100 million users in Africa (50 percent penetration of connected Africans), of which 80 percent access the social network on a mobile device. With much of the continent still using 2G service, Facebook has developed technology that identifies the user's network speed and adapts ads as needed.

One big impediment to mobile usage in developing economics has been the high price of smartphones. This is changing, and quickly. Google launched its Android One phone in India in 2014; this model retails for about $100. Another new smartphone launched in India, by Intex Technologies and its partner, Mozilla, retails for 1,900 rupees—or about $33. Xioami's Redmi and Motorola's Moto G devices are also lowering prices dramatically for smartphone consumers in India. Some 650 million Indians already own mobile devices, making India the second-largest mobile market globally, and the growth in smartphone ownership will pick up as affordability continues to increase.

● The Impact of the Mobile Economy

The mobile Internet is already generating some $700 billion in revenues annually—the equivalent of $780 for every adult—in the 13 countries that make up our sample. The mobile Internet has also created approximately 3 million jobs in these countries.

Both revenues and jobs are growing as mobile access expands and people do more things with a widening selection of devices. Mobile has only touched the surface in multiple industries that have an enormous impact on GDP—health care, for example. The Internet of Things and machine to machine (M2M) communications—two areas where the mobile Internet is cxpected to have widespread impact—are only in their infancy.

The mobile Internet attracts substantial investment. For example, leading app-store operators paid developers more than $15 billion between June 2013 and July 2014. Major companies, from telecommunications and cable service providers (Verizon, Comcast, and AT&T, for example) to hardware, software, and semiconductor manufacturers (Hewlett-Packard, Microsoft, Qualcomm) to content providers such as Netflix and Pandora, invest billions of dollars in R&D and capital expenditures, and countless start-ups are also attracting investments, innovating, and launching new products.As the volume of mobile traffic and activity relentlessly expands, the complexity of the industry that transports and delivers millions of terabytes of information every day increases dramatically as well. The industry is evolving rapidly. Competition within and among ecosystems is fuelling innovation, diversity, and choice for end users.

● Competition Drives Mobile Internet Growth

In both developed and developing markets, mobile usage is growing fast as consumers shift their online media consumption, commerce, information seeking, and social networking, among other activities, from fixed to mobile devices. Increasing mobile access everywhere is leading to new uses of the Internet—in fields from banking to education and from health care to the delivery of public services—further propelling its growth. Companies, governments, schools, hospitals, not-for-profits, and NGOs, among other organizations, increasingly realize that they need to interact with their stakeholders not just online but via smartphones and tablets. It is only a matter of time (and perhaps not much time) before the Internet becomes a mostly mobile phenomenon.

However, mobile internet revenues are growing fast. The revenues generated by the mobile Internet ecosystem are a big contributor to global GDP. We estimate that in 2013, they amounted to $682 billion in the 13 countries that account for approximately 70 percent of global GDP, or a substantial portion of the $2.9 trillion a year in revenues generated by all mobile technologies worldwide. (See Exhibit 3.) Smartphone users in the U.S. currently spend an average of $1,450 per year on their phones, data plans, apps, and content. Their European counterparts spend $740 per year, while in the Japanese market, annual per user spending amounts to $1,220 (The Mobile Internet Ecosystem Generated $682 Billion in Revenue in 2013 - Connected World: Growth of the Global Mobile Internet Econom)

By 2017, we estimate that mobile Internet revenues will have grown to $1.55 trillion across these 13 countries, an annual increase of 23 percent. Even in the economies where the mobile ecosystem is most mature, such as Japan and South Korea, annual growth will still be around 10 percent. In the major economies of the U.S., China, and the EU5, growth will be around 25 percent a year or more. The single largest contributor in the future will be apps, content, and services, fueled by the rapid expansion of mobile shopping and advertising.

The Mobile Internet Creates Jobs. Revenues are only one part of the picture. The mobile Internet is a major job-growth engine as well. We estimate that it has created employment for about 3 million people in the 13 countries we studied. Many of these jobs are in Asia, where the manufacturing of mobile devices is centered. But the rapid growth in device sales has also generated retail jobs throughout the U.S. and Europe, as well as in other regions. Network and infrastructure installation and maintenance take place worldwide. Jobs related to mobile operating systems and enablement platforms, which handle everything from hosting to security to billing and payment, are based primarily in the U.S. and Europe. Most employment is associated with devices and with apps, content, and services. These jobs tend to be created in countries with well educated and skilled workforces, and their numbers will grow as activity in these and other segments of the ecosystem expands. A significant proportion of these positions are entrepreneurial and situated in small enterprises—young (or maybe not so young) men and women hoping to impress users with the next big thing and hiring others when they do.

With revenues across the mobile Internet ecosystem forecast to more than double by 2017, there will be a related—and a significant, if not a proportional—increase in the number of jobs generated. Some of these will replace jobs currently found in the broader Internet ecosystem—for example, positions related to earlier generations of feature phones, particularly in developing economies. We also expect a substantial number of new jobs to be created as the demand for apps, content, and services rises disproportionately with the increase in the installed user base. The advent of new apps that automate and enhance existing activities, in fields such as health care and education, should help fuel this growth. Many of these jobs will require a high level of technical skill and creativity, and it will be important for governments to support appropriate education, training, and mobility programs to ensure that their workforces are in a position to take advantage of the opportunities that will be generated by the mobile Internet.

● Growth in Developing Markets

Rapid growth in developing markets stems from fast-rising penetration rates and increasing 3G and 4G coverage, both of which are propelling growth in apps, content, and services. India is growing at almost 40 percent annually; China and Brazil are growing at more than 25 percent a year. This growth is having a measurable impact on GDP, a direct effect on employment, investment, and consumption, and an indirect impact on productivity, entrepreneurship, and information flow. (See "Developing-Market Snapshot: The Mobile Internet in Brazil.")

● DEVELOPING-MARKET SNAPSHOT: THE MOBILE INTERNET IN BRAZIL

Analysis by the Group Speciale Mobile Association (GSMA) shows that a 10 percent increase in mobile broadband penetration raises GDP by 1.4 percent in low- and middle-income nations. A doubling in mobile data use increases GDP per capita by 0.5 percentage points. Faster connections also bring benefits. A 10 percentage point increase in 3G versus 2G use raises per capita GDP by 0.15 percentage points. None of this, however, reflects the economic impact of local entrepreneurs' ability to take their ideas global and generate increased revenues through their access to new customers and markets, a transformative benefit for small and medium-size businesses. (See "A Chinese Game Developer Goes Global.")

Not all developing markets are experiencing similar levels of growth. The GSMA has identified two categories in the developing world. "Fast growers" include countries such as China and Brazil, where a quarter or more of mobile Internet connections are made on smart devices and where 3G networks are growing quickly. More than 100 million smartphones were sold in China in the second quarter of 2014, according to The Economist, and eight of the top ten smartphone manufacturers were Chinese companies. "Discoverers" include many countries in Africa and Southeast Asia where smart devices represent less than 10 percent of mobile connections, and 90 percent of users rely on 2G networks.

In the discoverer category, three hurdles to higher penetration rates are lack of affordability, limited network coverage, and an unfavorable investment climate, and these can be formidable. Low income levels in many developing markets are the largest constraint on adoption. Extending networks to rural areas with little or no infrastructure is costly and promises little financial payback, since populations in which incomes are low generate low returns. Unpredictable regulation, high taxes, and high spectrum prices raise costs and slow adoption. In these developing countries, in particular, governments that take the long view can realize significant benefits. For example, a number of countries have policies that encourage digital and mobile technologies to leapfrog those of nations with more developed tech industries. (See "South Korea: The Impact of Open Competition.")

● SOUTH KOREA: THE IMPACT OF OPEN COMPETITION

National broadband plans can have a big impact as well. Research by the International Telecommunication Union (ITU) and Cisco Systems shows that such plans lead to 7.4 percent higher mobile Internet penetration, on average. History also shows that competitive markets speed both broadband and mobile penetration. The ITU/Cisco study found that countries with competitive markets have mobile penetration rates that are 26.5 percent higher than average.

One of the biggest infrastructure constraints (common to both developed and developing markets) is the availability, allocation, and use of mobile spectrum—the bands of radio waves over which data and voice communications (as well as other over-the-air media) travel. Lack of harmonization at the regional and international levels—meaning, for example, that the same operator's 3G network operates on different bands of spectrum in different countries or in different regions of the same country—leads to significant inefficiencies and higher costs. The GSMA estimates that by 2020, better harmonization could add $370 billion to GDP and 112,000 new jobs in Latin America, and $49 billion to GDP and 506,000 jobs in sub-Saharan Africa. North Africa could realize an additional $50.5 billion in GDP and 4 million jobs by 2025.

Beyond the direct economic impact, there are also social benefits stemming from greater mobile Internet penetration and usage. These include improved education, health care, and nutrition. By 2017, better distribution of life-saving information could save 1 million lives in sub-Saharan Africa through avoided malaria, HIV, and perinatal conditions. Using mobile technologies to track food deliveries, monitor food temperature, and optimize delivery routes could save enough food to feed 40 million people (the population of Kenya) in 2017—simply through reduced spoilage.

● The App Economy development

Mobile apps—the software programs that perform designated functions on a mobile device—may be the fastest growth story in recent history. Originally designed primarily for productivity purposes (mobile calendars, for example) and information retrieval (e-mail), mobile apps quickly expanded into numerous other fields, including gaming, navigation, health and fitness, media consumption, communication, and commerce, to name a few.

Apps are coded by developers, many of whom are entrepreneurs, and they are sold through distribution platforms such as the Apple App Store, Google Play, the Windows Store, Amazon Appstore, and BlackBerry World. App developers have made 1.3 million apps available through both the App Store and Google Play, some 255,000 through the Windows Store, 240,000 through Amazon, and 130,000 through BlackBerry World. In 2013 alone, apps were downloaded 102 billion times globally (of which 9.2 billion downloads were of paid apps), a 60 percent increase over 2012. Downloads are forecast to rise to 269 billion (15 billion paid) by 2017. Although many apps are given away free of charge, app revenues in our 13-country sample will nearly triple, from $26 billion in 2013 to $76 billion in 2017.

Even with the astronomical growth in the app economy, many app developers still struggle to monetize their endeavors. The vast majority of app downloads continue to cost nothing: nine out of ten downloads in 2013 were free, and eight of the ten most-used apps globally are given away, although many popular "free" apps generate income through advertising or in-app purchases (of extra content such as bonus game levels).

Developers are faced with a challenging business environment: a hit-driven market, in which relatively few apps gain critical mass, and low barriers to entry, with copycats and knockoffs of successful apps an all too common phenomenon. Large developers backed with big resources can tilt the playing field by paying to advertise their apps through a variety of channels. As a result, many independent developers earn little. More than half of all developers earn less than $500 a month per app, and the top 1.6 percent of developers earn more than the other 98.4 percent combined.

App developers, along with others throughout the mobile ecosystem, face continuing challenges in such areas as security. Threats are on the rise. Reports of mobile malware rose 167 percent in the 12 months ending in June 2014, with some 15 million mobile devices reportedly infected in 2014, up from 11.3 million in 2013. Just as Windows has been the target of most malware aimed at desktop operating systems, the most popular mobile operating systems are targeted because they are where the largest number of users can be found. Fragmented open source code can be more vulnerable to malware, and third-party app stores are key targets. One response from entrepreneurial developers has been new apps designed to secure phones (such as MobileIron, Samsung Knox, and XenMobile), but these usually rely on installation and updating by users rather than by device manufacturers. There are signs that consumers are purchasing apps on the basis of security and privacy. Threema and Telegram are two popular chat apps that stress their encryption and security.

In the face of these and other challenges, developers are using a variety of strategies to adapt. For example, some are choosing to specialize, producing niche apps in narrow fields (such as wedding planning) where they can charge a premium. On average, developers that focus on "mass-market reach" apps earn half as much as developers that build niche apps for consumers willing to pay for the service. Building sustainable revenue models for independent developers continues to be a big challenge. We expect developers to focus on two primary approaches.

Advertising-Supported and "Freemium" Revenue Models. More and more advertiser spending will shift to mobile over time, as consumer usage continues to increase and targeting technology improves. Global mobile advertising revenues are expected to have reached $18 billion in 2014, up from $13.1 billion in 2013, and this growth will continue until 2017, when spending will exceed $41 billion. About 90 percent of Apple's global App

Store revenue in 2013 was attributable to freemium apps—which are free to download but can ultimately lead to in-app purchases—up from 77 percent in 2012. Freemium apps have demonstrated their profitability but some have also come under criticism for allowing users to incur unexpected costs, such as through any in-app purchases that they wind up making.

Building Apps for Others. One area where developers are demonstrating success is building apps for other businesses. Some 70 percent of developers say they are profitable when doing contract work for others. Demand for app development is growing as industrial applications increase. Companies often do not have their own in-house developer talent and are willing to pay for functionality that can increase sales and profits.Developers are finding new opportunities in the Internet of Things. Some 25 billion new IoT devices (including cars, heating and air-conditioning units, lighting systems, farm equipment, wearables, and security systems) will come online from 2015 to 2020, doubling the current number. (See "The Next Big Thing: The Internet of Things.")

A big area of potential growth is machine-to-machine communication—networked devices of all kinds, in such industries as automotive, consumer goods, and utilities, that exchange information and perform functions without the physical assistance of humans. An aircraft engine that monitors and reports operating data in-flight is one example; buses and trucks that continually report their location, speed, and other information is another. Research organization IDATE expects the M2M market to reach €40 billion by 2017, with Europe being the biggest geographic market in terms of revenue. The EU had 52 million M2M connections in 2012 (about a quarter of the global total), and these are expected to grow to 295 million in 2017 (30 percent of the global total). The revenue numbers measured in the previous chapter are large. But they pale in comparison with what must be considered the real value of the mobile Internet: what all this activity is worth to the end user. Consumers worldwide are the big winners here. And the margin of victory runs into the trillions of dollars.

On conclusion, consumers use their mobile devices for a wide variety of purposes. The most valued feature is still phone calls, but this is followed closely by Web browsing, searching the Internet, and e-mail. Mapping capabilities, social networking, and financial functions are also very popular.

It's no exaggeration to say that consumers everywhere have come to depend on the mobile Internet. Whether it's for communication, consumption, commerce, or information, they are loathe to give up the capabilities that the mobile Internet confers. Large majorities would forgo most offline media (the one exception is TV) before forgoing mobile Internet access. Substantial majorities are also willing to give up such luxuries as fast food, chocolate, alcohol, coffee, and movies.

● The Mobile Internet Ecosystem - Connected World: Growth of the Global Mobile Internet Economy

The economics and nature of competition vary considerably within layers of the stack. The app market, for example, is international in scope, but a significant portion comprises apps that are entirely local in nature (for such reasons as language and culture). There are several big, global names in content (music and video, for example), but also some strong national and regional players—as well as millions of users. (Dailymotion.com, a French video website, has 20 million unique visitors who generate 2.5 billion video views each month.) M-commerce has both big international names (Amazon and eBay are two) and strong local and regional flavors (such as Alibaba in China and Flipkart in India), thanks to differing consumer tastes and supply chain considerations. Traditional retailers are rapidly blurring the lines between digital and brick-and-mortar commerce, adding further complexity to the mobile stack. The enablement platforms layer consists of services such as ad placement, billing and payments, identity verification, and publishing tools; it involves global companies like SAP, Spring Wireless, IBM, and Woodwing. Likewise, device manufacturers tend to be global businesses, with a wide range of companies (Samsung, Apple, Lenovo, Huawei) competing across countries and regions. For legacy and regulatory reasons, the service providers—telcos—are primarily national or multilocal companies. Some are developing regional strength—four carriers are active across multiple European countries, for examp

Thus,the center layer of the mobile stack is occupied by the operating systems that make smartphones smart, and that enable the convergence of computing power and portability in tablets and turn wearables into something much more than a wristwatch or an article of clothing. This layer is particularly dynamic and fast changing. Understanding distinctions among the major operating systems, each of which has its own goals, strategies, and impact, is essential to grasping how the mobile Internet industry works.

Sources

Cisco Visual Networking index GSMA intelligence, 2014

U.S. Commerce Dept., for 1956 to 2008 & Forrester Research forecasts, for 2009 to 2016.

● Behavioral Economic Theory
Analyzes Smart Mobile Phone
Consumer Behaviors

In fact, addiction to smartphone usage is a common worldwide problem among adults, which might negatively affect their wellbeing. This study investigated the prevalence and factors associated with smartphone addiction and depression among a Middle Eastern population. Whether internet will bring negative emotion to influence mobile phone buyers' telephone choiccs ?

Why does internet can influence smart mobile phone consumers' purchase desire? Has internet have direct relationship to influence smart mobile phone buyers' purchase desires ? Can the smart mobile phone talking product still attract phone buyers' preference choice, if it lacks internet function? I shall apply behavioral economic theory to attempt to explain the reasons how and why internet has direct relationship to influence smart mobile buyers' preference talking product choice in this traditional home telephone talking product market as below:

Is the internet putting up a barrier between people, even in bed? Does internet influence mobile phone consumers have not choose to buy because they are influenced to use mobiles when they use mobile to link internet to see any movies, or phones or news and influence their sleeping time in habit and they won't have nervous to work or learn on day time. We compulsively carry our smartphones with us wherever we go. The classroom, the bathroom, the bedroom, the outdoors — our phone is always in hand as if it were some magic self-defense tool capable of protecting us from all that is evil in the world. It all happened so fast. We didn't have the time to set any boundaries for smartphone usage, and now we find ourselves unable to save our relationships and form meaningful interactions with those dear to us.Smartphones are very useful in many circumstances. However, although not ruining your relationships per se, they can harm it in devious ways.

A smartphone is a modern day distraction that is so common, it's hardly noticed any more. It accompanies us wherever we go, demanding our attention multiple times a day. A phone call, a Facebook notification. We become irrevocably immersed in our digital lives, prioritizing the virtual world over anything else. Is it really that important to Instagram your dinner, rather than actually savoring it and sharing your impressions – or maybe a forkful of the dish – with the person next to you?Smartphones get in the way of our relationships, making it impossible for us to wholeheartedly devote our attention to the present moment. As a result, we lose many moments of wonder that are unique and never to be lived again.

Addiction to smartphone usage is a common problem among adults worldwide. It manifests itself in the excessive usage of their phones, while engaged in other activities such as studying, driving, social gatherings and even sleeping. However, many people fail to realize that addiction to smartphone usage is a serious issue that can have a negative effect on the person's thoughts, behavior, tendencies, feelings, and sense of well-being. In particular, it can be a risk factor for depression, loneliness, anxiety and sleep disturbances. As per the Mental Health Foundation in the United Kingdom, people with depression experience an unhappy mood, loss of interest or pleasure, feelings of guilt or low self-worth, disturbed sleep or appetite, low energy, and poor concentration. Depressive and anxiety disorders are two main common disorders that are highly prevalent globally, as over 300 million people are estimated to suffer from depression, which is equivalent to 4.4% of the world's population. It is speculated that not only addiction to smartphone usage can affect one's mental and behavioral status, but also that those with mood disorders are more likely to become addicted to using their smartphones .

Numerous tools have been utilized in literature to assess the same phenomenon, but with different terms such as excessive smart phone usage, smartphone addiction, dependency on smart phones, internet addiction, problematic mobile phone usage, and so on. Remarkably, there was a tendency to use a non-pathological terminology, such as "Problematic Smartphone Use," rather than the term smartphone addiction. Addiction manifests itself in various forms such as preoccupation, tolerance, lack of control, withdrawal, mood modification, conflict, lies, excessive use and loss of interest. Several studies have found that women are more likely to develop an addiction to smartphone usage than men. This was viewed as a positive way for people to stay connected in social relationships. One study clarified that women like to show affection to their families using their smartphones while men use phones for efficiency and practicality . Though there are several studies on this topic, no study has proven this connection so far. Smartphone addiction has been found to be correlated with various physical and psychological issues, as indicated in a number of studies that tested this relationship among various age groups. For example, one study found that people with depression, social anxiety and loneliness had different uses for their smartphones compared to others. People with social anxiety made fewer outgoing calls, as well as, fewer text messages than those without social anxiety. It was reported that high levels of smartphone addiction were correlated with low self-esteem, loneliness, depression and shyness.

Although, internet can bring smart mobile phone users to spend sleeping time to use this kind of mobile product to watch movies, watch TV, listen music, social media communication, searching etc. non-talking communication behaviors. It seems that internet may influence smart phone users to change their phone purchase choice to buy the kind common mobile product more. But, in behavioral economic view, internet can bring smart mobile phone product has more attractive strengths to influence common mobile phone kind product users to chooce to use smart mobile phone products in preference. Internet can also bring these positive emotion to persuade the common mobile users to choose to use them.

Convenient applying: Any smart phone users can apply smart phone to link to internet to replace home computers to link to internet to watch movies, watch TV, listen music, social media communication, searching etc. non-talking communication behaviors in anywhere and any time conveniently. It is one kind of small size and light talking communication tool, but it can also help any mobile users to apply smart phone product to apply internet to do the same computer tasks in any time and any places. Hence, smart mobile can bring many computer users to feel that they can apply computer to do similar internet search behaviors at home. Convenient internet search function is one attract function to influence traditional computer users to choose to apply smart phone tools to replace computers tools to apply internet to search information, news, watch TV, movie, lisen music etc. social media communication behaviors at homes. When they bring smart phone to any where, then they can apply this tool to click to internet to do the same computer and internet link tasks in order to enjoy their entertainment needs. So, they do not need to apply computer tool to link to internet to enjoy their visal entertainment at homes. They can bring smart phone to go to anywhere to link to internet to enjoy their visal entertainment in any time conveniently. So, smart phone can be replaced to home computer tool to solve any visal entertainment enjoyers' needs.

● Internet brings smart phone users to feel more visal entertainment enjoyment

The Internet has revolutionized direct communication, lead to the digitization of books and film, as well as made convenience even more important. Companies have developed strategies that capitalize on the growing desire for easily accessible goods and services in only a few mouse clicks. As technology grows increasingly local and more connected to all aspects of the customer purchasing process, small business owners need to be more efficient in how they target their markets. Understanding why convenience plays such a large role in the purchasing process is vital in growing a successful business. Here are five trends that have popped up in recent years as businesses looked for ways to help their customers take advantage of well-timed opportunities. Internet can bring more attract to smart phone users, instead of visal enjoyment needs, the reasons may include as below:

1. Prior Consumer Knowledge

In today's digital world, consumers are looking for retail solutions which allow them to maximize their free-time and to stretch their disposable income. Due to this economic climate, small businesses which are able to provide their customer with a more convenient experience than a large retailer, are cashing in. H.M Cole, a custom clothier, offers its customers an entire planned wardrobe for the upcoming year after an hour's consultation. Other convenience services such as Trunk Club and Stitch Fix, personalized styling sites for men and women respectively, take that one step further in creating a complete look. These levels of convenience take a simple fitting and turn it into a way for consumers to spend less time deciding outfits, and more time doing other things they value.

2. Direct-to Store Delivery

Due to the "larger-than-life" nature of big box stores, they have begun to develop strategies which combat the convenience of a smaller retailer. The newest trend among these chains is to offer direct-to store delivery. Shoppers are able to find what they are looking for online, and purchase directly on the site. Rather than having to wait the 3-5 days for delivery, chains are making their purchases available (sometimes at discounted rates) for pick up at their local store. Essentially, customers are taking part in shopping services where the store physically groups together the inventory, saving the individual time in their purchases.

3. Personalized Billing, Shipping Info

Customer profiles across frequently visited webpages allow for consumers to not only keep their billing information in one place, but also have access to similar products or content. Businesses are able to not only track purchases, but to specifically target an individual with the information provided for convenience sake. A user does not usually choose to re-enter billing or shipping information on a site they frequent, and so by saving this information, a company is removing an obstacle that might otherwise influence the purchase.

4. Time is Money

Fast food and drive-thru options have changed the world's nutritional demands, creating a society of cheap convenience foods. Although the nutritional value of these highly-processed foods is lacking, the demand for them has been on the rise across the globe. While these types of businesses are growing at a record rate, the pressure to remain affordable and convenient has driven them online.

Some innovative restaurant chains have transitioned to online ordering which provide an easy, personalized interface for their customers to select and buy all from the website portal. A restaurant receives the order digitally, packages the food, and then sends it out to delivery, often for an additional fee. Both Google and Amazon , as well as many startups, have launched services that deliver meals and groceries to your home. Time has shown that customers are willing to spend a little more for the convenience of having food arrive at their doorstep.

5. Subscription Services

Another recent convenience service trend is through subscription services. This can include streaming goods such as TV shows, movies, audio books, or music tracks. Companies charge their customers a fee to have access to a database of content whenever, wherever they want. Some providers have included commercials as a means to generate more income. Other subscription services include coffee of the month clubs, or deliver gift boxes. These companies charge a monthly (or yearly) subscription fee and compile a box of themed goodies for their customers.While some very big companies have struggled to make convenience a larger part of their customers' experiences, many small businesses that offer niche products and services have an advantage in this area. The Internet is helping them to level the playing field in a way. It provides a platform for small businesses to capitalize on the demand for goods by using convenience to win fans and new customers.

On conclusion, internet can bring smart phone users to do any activities when they need to apply computer tools at home in any time and anywhere. So, internet has direct relationship to persuade mobile phone or computer users to choose to buy in preference nowadays.

Reference

Bigne, Enrique (2005). The impact of internet user shopping patterns and demographics on consumer mobile buying.

Falk, Louis, K. et. al (2005) " E-commerce and consumer's expectations: What makes a website work". Journal of website promotion, 1(1), 65-75.

Parasuraman, A., Zeithaml, V.A. and Berry L.L. (1988) SERVQUAL: A multiple-item scale for measuring consumer perceptions of service quality. Journal of retailing, 64, 12-40.

CHAPTER FIVE

Technology marketing economy Development

Future when the thinking capabilities of computers approach our own is quickly coming into view. Raid process in coming decades will bring about machines with human –level intelligence capable of speech and reasoning, with a myriad of contributions to economics, politics and warcraft. The birth of true artificial intelligence will profoundly affect humankind's future. In our future technological development market, what it will bring much influences to economy. I shall indicate these several aspects, they may include as below:

On artificial intelligent invention brings high unemployment to low skill employees aspect, from the time the last artificial intelligence break through was reached in the last 1940s, scientists around the world have looked for ways of this " artificial intelligence" to improve technology, raising efficiency and productivity beyond what even the most sophisticated of today's artificial intelligence programs can achieve. Even now, research is ongoing to better understand what the new AI programs will be able to do, when remaining within the intelligence such as human brain. Most AI programs currently programmed have been limited primarily to making simple decisions or performing simple operations on relatively small amounts of data.

AI technological invention will bring much contribution to influence our future economic development. It had unique characteristics to compare common machines and it can help many industries to raise efficiency, productivity and improve performance as well as consumer individual self use. Such as the network is not taught to understand prose in any human sense. Instead, during its training phase, it adjusts the internal connections in its simulated neural networks to best anticipate the next word. It can be applied to read any article and understand any meaning to write any article as same to authors' mind and writing ability. For example, in the future, any one entered the first few sentences of any article, you are reading, the algorithm spewed out two paragraphs that sounded liked a freshman's effort to recall the gist of an introductory lecture on machine learning during which she was daydreaming. The output contains all the right words and phrases , not bad. So, (AI) technology can be applied to become just one more example of programs that do things thought to be uniquely human playing the real-time strategy game, translating text, making personal recommendations for books and movies, recognizing people in images and videos. But with the invention, of deep neural networks and the massive computational of the tech industry, computers improved until their outputs to longer appeared . In the future, algorithms can best humans, (AI) can help human to do any things in possible. Then, our society will encounter one automobile machine working environment. Does (AI) innovation will low skill employees lose their jobs because robotic can replace to any human to do simple jobs in any industries.

Whether machines can become sentient matters for ethical reasons. If computers experience life through their own senses, they cease to be purely a means to an end determined by their usefulness to us humans. Then our society will have many jobs which are needed to be worked by human, due to (AI) or robotic invention, it can replace human to do many simple jobs, e.g. factory manufacturing jobs, warehouse deliver jobs, public transportation , e.g. tram, train, ferry, underground train, bus etc. driving tasks, they are replaced by robotic auto driving, even pilot flying job will be also replaced to drive air planes by (AI) driving on sky impossible. Although, (AI) can help businesses to raise efficiency, increase productivity and improve performance, but it also bring these jobs to be replaced by (AI) and it will cause many people lose jobs when (AI) is invented to be applied in popular in our future societies. On business benefits aspect, (AI) can bring working efficiency and productivity improvement, but it can also bring unemployment ratio raises as the same time when employers accept to apply (AI) to replace human to any simple or difficult tasks.

So, we need to limit or prohibit (AI) invention to exceed human's extent in possible. I mean that we do not need to limit to invent any (AI) skill, but we need to concern human need to work in the same time. If (AI) was real replaced to do any simple jobs in any industries, then there are many low skill workers , such as factory workers, clean workers, drivers ,even high skill workers, such as lawyer, teacher, pilot. They will lose their jobs in possible. So, how to invent (AI) technology will influence our future global employment chance to provide us to continue to work in any organizations. So, (AI) will may bring high unemployment ratio, if it is applied to any low skill , even high skill jobs aspects to different industries in global.

On conclusion , in economist view, technology market development must need, such as (AI) invention because it can help any industries to raise efficiency, productivity and improve performance, but we need to know how it can be applied to avoid human to lose jobs, due to (AI) is replaced to do their tasks for any industries in possible. Whether (AI) invention can create jobs or bring job lose? (AI) scientists must need to consider how to invent their skill to be applied to which tasks aspect if they hope human won't lose many jobs to do in future one day.

- How to apply robotic to raise efficiency and productivity and improving performance for manufacture as well as bringing long term productive economic benefit to manufacturers?

It is one good question. Can scientists only concentrate on researching artificial intelligent for raising productivity, efficiency and improving performance to businesses aspect, so neglecting on research other scientific researching aspects? Technological marketing economy is as a play between independent individual subjects. However, it has also become clear that the notion of play has to be interpreted within a different framework than that of classical functionalism. In mainstream classical economics, interaction or exchange is understood as the effect of the ends-means rationally of individuals. Smith's sympathy –based view of man and society avoids this functionalistic reduction of interaction and exchange. For example, the utilitarian or functional aspect of , the social process of producing and distributing wealth through free exchange, is in Smith's view on part of the value and belief system which people in ordered and prosperous societies employ to give sense and meaning to their experiences.

Hence, in our business society, technology can bring marketing economic change to be better. One free technology marketing economic society must have these advantages to bring to influence our living, such as below:

It interprets and explains improving social processes of producing and distributing to business, such as (AI) skill invention , it can help businesses to improve performance and efficiency and productivities for their manufacturing aim only, but (AI) ought not be applied to replace to do all low skill workers' jobs in any positions in any factories or warehouses. So, any employers ought not dismiss all workers and they are replaced by all robotics. They will need to consider overall economic benefit. I mean that avoiding low skill workers unemployment ratio raises. For example, one factory can still keep 50% workers and 50% robotics to cooperate to work together. Because some human workers can be such as assistants to do any simple tasks in factory every teams. Human workers can discover any errors to let manager to know in order to improve in their cooperation process with robotics. So, human workers and robotics cooperation , it is more efficient manufacturing method to compare any manufacturing process is needed to finish from robotics only in any future factory or warehouse working environment. So, robotics and human workers cooperation can bring the most efficient production and distribution benefits to future manufacturers in any factories or warehouses because human can help robotics to find any error in order to improve. Otherwise, if the factory or warehouse has only all robotics to work. Although, they may bring raising productivities or improving performance and efficiencies. But they can not know whether how to improve their errors or revises their every time productive performance to be better every day. SO, the most efficient manufacturing method is that human workers and robotics cooperate to work together in any factories or warehouses.

On innovation and information economic influence aspect, one of the most important topics in economics is the economics of information. Information includes things as varied as e-mail, and even the text book you are reading. Information is a very different kind of commodity from things like pizza and shoes because information is expensive to produce , but cheap to reproduce. Because of the unusual nature of information, it is subject to market failure, so we need to develop different kinds of public politics to regulate it, the law of " intellectual property".

We are encountering the essence of economic development is innovation and that monopolists are in fact of innovation in a capitalist economy. What does the economics of information mean ? Who do we need to develop information economy? Modern economics emphasizes the special problems involved in the economics of information. Information is a fundamentally different commodity from normal goods. Because information is costly to produce , but cheap to reproduce, markets in information are subject to serve market failures.

For the production of software program industry example, the windows software, developing this program took several years and cost Microsoft many money of dollars. You can purchase a legal copy for $5. The same phenomenon is at work in pharmaceutical, entertainment and other areas where much of the value of a good comes from the information it contains. In each of these areas, the research and development to software on the product may be an expensive process that takes years. But once, the information is recorded on paper, in a computer or on a compact disc, it can be reproduced and used by a second person essentially for free.

The inability of firms to capture the full monetary value of their invention is called inappropriability. Inventions are not fully appropriable because other firms may imitate an invention, in which case the other firms may derive some of the benefits of the inventive investments. Sometimes, imitators may drive down the price of the new product, in which case consumers would get some of the rewards. Information consumers can earn these benefits when the value of an invention to all consumers and producers is many times the appropriable private return to the inventor (the monetary value of the invention to the inventor).

However, information is expensive to produce but cheap to reproduce. To the extent the rewards to invention are inappropriable, we would expect private research and development to be underfunded, with the most significant underinvestment in basic research because that is the least appropriable kind of information. The inappropriability and high social return on research can lead most governments to subsidize basic research in the fields of health and science and to provide special incentives for other creative activities. Thus, special laws governing patents, copyrights, business and trade secrets and electronic media create intellectual property rights. The purpose is to give the owner special protection against the material's being copied and used by others without compensation to the owner or original creator.

On the Internet information economic market influence hand, inventions that improve communications are hardly limited to the modern age. But the rapid growth of electronic storage, access and transmission of information highlights of providing incentives for creating new information. Many new information technologies have large sunk costs but virtually zero marginal costs. With the low cost of electronic information systems like the internet, it is technologically possible to make the large amounts of information available to everyone, everywhere, at close to zero marginal cost. Perfect competition is nowadays different e-commerce internet information business competitive feature, and any e-commerce merchants can not survive here because a price equal to a zero marginal cost will yield zero revenues and therefore no viable firms.

Hence, the economics of the information economy highlights the conflict between efficiency and incentives. On the one hand, all information ,might be provided free of charge, e.g. free e-book download, e-song download e-movie download from internet. Free provisions of information looks economically efficient because the price would thereby be equal to the marginal cost, which is zero. But a zero price on intellectual property would destroy the profits and therefore reduce the incentives to produce new books from authors, movies and songs from creators would earn little rewards from their creative activity. But with the costs reproduction and transmission so much lower for electronic information than for traditional information, so the future any electronic publishing industry 's products, e.g. e-books, e-songs , e-music, e-movies prices will be lower than traditional paper books, pack of songs and movies price, either consumers go to shops to buy them or consumers pay visa card to enter websites to buy any e-books , songs, e-music , e-movies from internet channel. Then, it will cause these traditional publishing and entertainment industries' competition to be raised because these e-publishers or e-entertainment can reduce their price to sell from their websites when their costs are nearly to zero. Hence, information technology can raise competition to the traditional publishing and entertainment industries. The traditional paper book, music, movie business merchants need to any authors or creators to help them to create any unique movies, songs, paper books to sell from their shops and they need to ensure their authors or music , movie creators won't give these creative book, song, movie products to any e-music, e-publisher, e-movie merchants to sell from their websites absolutely.

On conclusion, information technology influence any music, publish, movie creative product competitive raising to the traditional paper book publishers, music or movie publishers when many book publishers or music or movie creators choose e-commerce to replace traditional shop visiting sale method. So , it is possible to influence overall publishing and music and movie creative industries will change to e-commence consumption model. Then the traditional book and music and movie visiting stores will disappear and the online websites to these merchants will increase and their price also will reduce in global e-publishing and e-creative product consumption environment. So, information technology will bring some traditional store visiting number decreases and online merchant e-store number increases and consumers can pay less price to buy these creative products from internet.

● Software entertainment game strategy influences economic growth

What is information technologic game strategy? How and why information technological game strategy can influence economic growth? I shall explain as below:

Nowadays, Macrosoft and Microcorp are the global information technological big companies. They own much market share in global information technological industry. Whether what factors influence they can still be global information technological products leaders. Why does computer software consumers still choose their products to compare other software products in preference? I suppose that Macrosoft and Microcorp, their hypothetical any software games have developed a clever new computer game that is certain to be very popular. Although Microcorp have the unique competitive advantage with its own software game engineers and compete against Macrosoft, but it can so it cheaper and better if it can hire any Macrosoft's software game engineers. So, in economic view, it needs to pay high salary (higher cost) to hire Macrosoft's engineers (labor), but Macrosoft's engineers can help Microcorp to invent any new kinds of software games to compete Macrosoft. Although, Microsorp needs to pay higher labor cost, but when it can raise its any software games' design and game playing methods to attract any game players. Then, these new and exciting software games can help it can bring many game entertainment players and then it can sell cheaper price to raise more attractive effort to win its competitor (Macrosoft). So, higher software game designing engineers (skill labor), their game designing effort will be the major factor to influence any one information technological companies in success. If one software designing company can employ one high software game designing effort profession to help it to design any kinds of attractive software games. Although, it may pay high salary (labor cost), but it have much chance to attract many software game buyers to compare that if it pays less salary to employ one poor game software designing profession. Because the poor software game designing profession may need to spend long time to research how to design any kinds of attractive game software to excite game players' playing desires in this playing software game industry market. Long time research to the poor software game designer may be one none any reward to compensate to the software game designing firm when it needs to pay long time salary to employ him. Otherwise, if the software game designing firm can accept to pay higher salary to the higher software game designer, he will have higher chance to help it to design any more attractive software games to influence game players' playing game entertainment desires. So, any software game designing companies their game designers (labor) must be the major factor to influence their business succeeds or fails in this software game entertainment market.

On the employing method hand, Microcorp can choose to include in its contracts with its software engineers that from working for another Macrosoft software company for a certain period of time if they resign from Macrosoft. A move such as this is sometimes called a preeptive move. Its propose is to alter its rivals' payoffs in order to alter their employing strategies. Preemptive moves are usually costly (high slaary), and this one is no exception. In its employment contracts makes Macrosoft a less attractive to let its old game software engineers want to leave their current employer, such as Macrosoft. As a result, Macrosoft must pay its software game designing engineers above the going market salary if it hopes their employment contracts can be continue between Macrosoft and its software game engineers.

Should Macrosoft must need to decide how to react. It can choose to fight Microcorp by aggressively advertising its game, which is costly high, but gives it a larger market share in the game player entertainment market, when Macrosoft had any one profession game software engineer(s) leave(s) his company and he/they change(s) to the another Microcorp software game designing company to work, or it can forego the expense of an advertisement campaign and simply share the market 50/50 with its major competitor, Microcorp to be partners.

Their competition has close relationship to influence economic growth because it will have many game players number to be increase if they can cooperate to be partners in success when they can design any new kinds of software game products to satisfy software game players' entertainment feeling. Otherwise, if they can not be one good partners and they only consider their every business benefits and neglect themselves business benefits. Then, their software playing games sale price can either to be reduced in order to attract any software game players when their software games can not be designed to have much new playing methods to attract many game players. Consequently, the GDP income to this software game entertainment market must reduce because any kinds of entertainment software games prices are reduced as well as the game players number is also decreasing. Due to they are the major software entertainment game suppliers in global. Any game players will only choose either Microcorp or Macrosoft to buy their any kinds of entertainment software game products to play majorly. So, their software game manufacturing and sale number must influence global GDP income increases or decreases in macro economy view. It implies that any countries technological software game industry's GDP income will depend on these both Microcorp and Macrosoft software game's cooperation relationship whether they have good or bad cooperation relationship. If their cooperation relationship is good, then they can manufacture high quality and attractive entertainment software games as well as raising sale price and exciting many game players' entertainment desires to achieve the increase to game players number aim more easily.

How to achieve their cooperation relationship more easier. I suppose that, in the software game entertainment industry, over its lifetime, the computer game will generate $500,000 in new income (income minus production cost) for all the firms producing it or its clones. Macrosoft must pay its software engineers an additional $100,000 to get them to agree to accept a contract containing an anticompetition clause. It costs Microcorp $100,000 to develop the software if it can hire Macrosoft's engineers and $200,000 otherwise. Aggressive advertising costs Macrosoft $70,000 and has the effect of giving it a 80% market share if it restricts its engineers' employment and a 72% market share if it does not. So, the fall in total market share is caused by the fact that without some of Macrosoft's advertisements. If however, Macrosoft passively acquiesces to Microcorp's entry and shares the market, then both firms can still achieve a 50% market share fairly. Hence, they must need to achieve 50/50 market share if they hope to achieve the cooperation relationship in success. Otherwise, they will not achieve cooperation relationship in success.

However, the spending advertisement factor will also their cooperation chance in success. For example, it would be more realistic to recast the Software Game as one in which Macrosoft chooses how much to spend on advertising with sales depending continuously on the amount spent. Other examples of continuous cooperation choices may include: the productive capacity of an electrical power plant; the salary to offer a prospective employee; or the insurance premium to charge a prospective policyholder.

So, the amount to any of these expenditure factor will influence whether they will decide to cooperate to sell their software games products in global game entertainment market.
How and why Macrosoft and Microcorp's cooperation can influence global economic growth? It is significant that Macrosoft and Microcorp both technological software game designing companies are global the largest firms, they are doing international software game trade business to many countries and they have large market share in the software entertainment game sale market. Aside from trade based on technological gaps and software game product cycles, software game entertainment industry is dynamic in nature or game players' entertainment taste will change any time in completely static in nature. That is, given the nation's game players' playing taste and game entertainment factor, such as game playing designing technological method and game player individual playing game taste both. We proceeded to determine the nation's comparative advantage and the gains from the different kinds of entertainment software game designing supply factor and the game player individual game taste changing factor. So, any nation's software game players number will depend on these both factors to influence whether their number will either increase or decrease in the year in this global software game entertainment market. However, these factors can be changed by time, technology usually can improve any software game playing methods and game player individual playing taste will also change any time. As a result, the nation's comparative advantage also changes over time, such as when the nation has many game players lose their interest to buy any software games to play, then the nation ought not only consider how to develop its software entertainment game in the technological industry, it is right time to research any other new technological industries to develop if it still hopes its GDP income can rise in the technological industry overall aspect. Such as dynamic trade theory is still in its infancy. However, our comparative statics analysis can carry us a long way in analyzing the effect on international trade resulting from changes in factor technology, and tastes over time, such as entertainment software game case.
The growth of factors of production will also influence the software game entertainment industry development, through time, a nation's population usually grows and with its size of its labor force , such as China and India. Similarly, by utilizing part of its resources to produce capital equipment, e.g. India needs to utilize its technological resources, technological engineers

and technological material can need to be used to manufacture either new software game products or computers. But, its technological resources will be shortage (both labor and technological material). So, many technological companies choose to apply more technological material and technological engineers to use much time and money to manufacture any new software game products. Then, these labor and material resources will be reduced to be spent time and material to manufacture any new computer products in the year. In this technological industry case, capital refers to all the man-made means of production, such as machinery, factories, communication and education and training of labor force, all of which greatly enhance the nation's ability to produce either computer products or software game products. So, the national will also continue to assume that it can experiencing economic growth is producing two commodities, such as software game and computer both kinds of technological products under the constant returns to scale. So, if India can not raise the rapid technical process to skill labor and supply technological material supplying number to satisfy to manufacture the enough software game and computer products to supply them to sell to any countries' playing game players and computer users every month. Then, its technological industry will lose many clients, due to it can not supply enough software games and computers number to sell to any countries.

Several empirical studies have indicated that most the increase in real per capita income in technological industrial nations is due to technical progress and much less to capital accumulation. However, the analysis of technical progress is much more complex than the analysis of factor growth because there are several definitions and types of technical progress, and they can take place at different rates in the production of either or both commodities, such as software game and computer.

Technical progress is usually classified into neutral, labor saving , or capital saving. All technical progress , regardless of its types reduces the amount of both labor and capital required to produce any given level of output. So, if India could have good technical progress to raise its technological labor skill and reducing the technological material to be used to manufacture the software games and computers. Then, it will have chance to keep the maximum manufacturing level number to software game and computer products as the same time.

CHAPTER SIX

Scientific technology influences economy development

Any countries must have limited skill labor and technological materials to manufacture any high technological products. Nowadays, information technology and technology both industries are increasing needs to adapt consumers' need to enjoy to use any kinds of technological products in order to satisfy their better living of standard feeling. However, any countries' technological engineers number and technological material number, they have limited number to supply to any technological industries to use to manufacture any high technological products. In economic view, comparative advantage will cause when the technological product manufacturer needs to employ technological engineers skill labors and technological material to choose to manufacture either any related information technological products or general technological products, such as the skill labor and technological material supply number is limited. If the technological product manufacturer choose to apply more skill labors and technological matieral to manufacture any information technological product. Then, due to skill labors and techological material supplying number shortage factor, I believe that they will not have enough skill labor and technological material to supply to manufacture any high technological products. Hence, they must need to compare whether information technological product or other technological product both kinds, which kind of technological product can help them to bring more economic manufacturing benefit in order to sell to global technological product market. I shall indicate the technology product, such as natural energy, farming technology etc. as well as automatic technology in manufacturing industry to let manufactures to compare whether they ought choose apply technological skill labor and technological material to choose to use to manufacuture information technological product, such as (AI)smart mobile, (AI) smart mobile game software or other technological products in order to bring more comparative economic benefit to themselves.

The future comparative economic advatanges between information technology and technology products may include as below:

(1) Information technological related online distance learning teaching service provision to students' learning need

High level education and high birth

rate population raising online learning information technology distance learning service needs.

According to John G. (2016) indicated that " a point forecast is that GDP per capita will rise well under 1% per year in the longer run, with overall GDP growth of a little over 1 to 12%. The main drivers of slow growth are educational attainment and demographics. First, rising educational attainment will add less to productivity growth than it did historically. Second because of the aging and retirement of baby boomers, employment will rise more slowly than population which in turn, is projected to rise slowly relative to history." Thus, it seems that some economists believe education and born rate will influence future US employment method. They assume that the employment and growth ratio will rise and unemployment ratio will deadline of US will increase birth ratio and future there are many young people (students) can have chance to accept high education degree to raise whose education level to prepare to enter different kinds of high educational jobs market to work in the future.

Considering a more growth accounting perceptive on productivity growth. According to the analysis in Fernald (2015) which uses a multi-sector growth model for the projections. It indicated that although, the details differ and if bases projections on TFP data since 2004, it also implies a preferred point estimate of 1.6% per year in US over this short period. The " fundamentals" of labor-productivity growth (namely, growth in total factor productivity , TFP) have exceeded the actual realization for reasons that reflect the unwinding of dynamic of labor quality and capital depending associated with the great recession. Thus, how to raise labor quality which concerns how to raise educational level to young people in any country will be one labor economic challenge in US in the future.

Fernald (2015) also explained " the shortfall" in productivity growth relative to fundamentals reflects, at least in part, the unwinding of two dynamics associated with the great recession. He indicated that first, at the end of the great recession business had a lot of capital relative to labor, which has attended the need of add capacity to meet demand in recent years. In contrast to the outsized growth in capital deepening from 2007 to 2010 year, we have seen capital "shallowing" since 2010 year. Second, businesses fired low-skilled workers during the recession, which raised labor quality in 2007 year to 2010 year period. As these potential workers have been rehired, the growth rate of labor quality has added less.

Thus, on the one hand, when one country encounters economic recession, many employers will like to employ high educational level and high skilled labor to raise productivity. If US encountered economic recession, but it had none (lacked) enough high educational level and high skilled knowledgeable workers to be supplied to the labor market in US. Then, US will encounter long term economic recession period, it can't shorten economic recession period. Thus, US will need to let many US young people have effort to study to prepare enough high educational level knowledge to do different kinds of professional or high knowledgeable or high technological jobs in future US labor market.

However, US high knowledgeable labor can also assist US businessmen to raise productivity growth. Due to labor quality could be grown by high educational and increasing number of knowledgeable workers. On the other hand, moreover, if there are many US young married parents who will either choose not born any babies for next generation or choose born only one to four children. Then, future US will have a small numbers of young people to be supplied to primary schools, high schools, even universities to study. It also means the university level graduate student numbers will decrease also. So, low birth rate factor can also influence the high knowledgeable labor numbers to be supplied to future US labor market. So, I recommend that US government needs to encourage many young parents choose born next generation and provides student loans to lend to poor families to support whose children can have more chance to attempt to go to high schools or universities to study in the future

Future, online teaching method will be popular to be applied to teach to any university, even secondary and primary schools. Because internet service is free charge to any students in any countries. Many different age students who can know how to apply internet as well as internet studying is very convenient to any students who can to internet to learn or study in home or public library or school library conveniently. Teachers do not need spend much time to teach students in classroom. They can use internet to teach teachers by face to face seeing and talking to their individual student from every student's computer. So, students do not also often spend much time to go to school to learn. So, developing any fast speed and time saving and talking and listening online teaching methods will be popular needs to any UK primary and secondary and university students in the future. It will be one new technological teaching method to change the traditional classroom educational method in UK and schools. For example, when one UK student who had left UK and is living in another country long time. If any UK school did not provide online teaching service to any UK students. It means that the UK citizen can not choose study himself/herself any UK school if who still hope to study any UK course when who is living in another country. Even one foreign student who does not go to UK to study, if he/she can find any UK primary or secondary or university to study from online. Then, the UK school won't lose one foreign student, due to it does not provide online teaching method to any foreign students. So, online Technology educational learning method will be one popular learning method which is enhanced, supported, mediated or assessed by the use of electronic media. Technology also enhanced learning may involve the use of new or established technology and/or the creation of new learning material. It may be deployed both locally and at a distance (i.e. a combination of traditional and e-learning approaches), to learning that is delivered entirely online. Online learning technology characteristics (features) include identification of a project lead for each area of any learning strategy, identification of two " quick win" for example lecture capture, electronic submission and feedback.

How can online technology enhance learning at UK any schools? It will include these several aspects to analyze. On identifying, prioritizing and innovation hand, online technology is a process for resourcing, prioritizing, acquiring and evaluating school software and hardware for UK any school needs. On staff development learning plan and a student skills development plan hand, UK schools need to establish a base-line policy on the standard (minimum) technology enhanced learning expectation for education each program and module and a mechanism for updating the schools' policies. On evaluation and research hand, a mechanism for engaging the owners of the technology enhanced learning strategy with best practice in the sector including contributing to and benefiting from pedagogical research and the evaluation of the student experience to UK any school.

Thus, UK schools can apply online technology to develop on educational aspect, such as digital literacies and appropriate technical skills that equip UK students for life-long learning, graduate level employment and professional practice, be empowered to learn how to learn with online teaching technology, using online technology to engage in interactive, creative and co-constructed learning with the potential for online learning in an interdisciplinary and international context, using online teaching technology to engage in learning with and from people from anywhere in the world, be supported on placement and in workplace learning through mobile applications and other supportive technologies that facilitate their online learning when away from the classroom, having access to innovative methods of online learning teaching and assessment that are the foundation of a research-lead academic environment, engaging with UK schools in developing , implementing and reviewing the technology enhanced learning strategy. Thus, in the future, it is important to build a capacity to the online education strategy to adopt future learning innovation and student individual online learning need (demand) to UK any school online teaching trend.

There are many examples where UK academics working in isolation or in small UK teaching organizations or classroom learning groups have developed teaching innovation that have a positive impact on UK students' academic experience , but these have remained isolated to particular modules or occasionally program. The aim of education researching online learning process is to identify the good online teaching innovation that is being developed and to prioritize those that have the potential to make a significant contribution to improving the academic student experience at UK any schools. This online teaching process will need any UK schools which can plan how to apply limited resources necessary to achieve online teaching. In addition, the online teaching research process would evaluate and prioritize large scale educational software and hardware requests for primary, secondary and university students' requests. An important part to this process will be to ensure the integration of online educational products and packages that school staff and students regular use to make routine working and access as seamless as possible.

Decisions about school administrative online technologies should not be taken in isolation before assessing the impact on UK teaching staff. In addition, a range of techniques such as, online expert facilitation, coaching and peer support will be used to support individuals, groups or longer academic units, who are learning on major technology enhanced online learning projects. Staff engagement may also facilitated through incorporating technology that is used in teaching staff research and/or professional activity that can be cooperated into their teaching.

Online learning technology can develop UK students skills, UK schools need to understand how UK students understand technology and learn with it, therefore the digital literacy strategy needs to be considered as part of the overall strategy as well as the relevant skills development in UK employability strategy. So, in the future, online learning strategy will make it clear that students will develop technical skills the appropriate level for graduate employability and professional practice. Also, in the future, the online technology can enhance learning working group to discuss external development, that are of educational strategic importance, understanding and evaluating current best practice and research and understanding and evaluating the online educational strategic contribution that pedagogical research and student feedback can have on online educational strategy, policy and practice. The e-learning unit is responsible for informing and educating. This could be done by, for example, providing a short digest of relevant information for each meeting and by setting aside a proportion of each school meeting to discuss a topic of particular online educational strategic interest to every school. Academics that have not got a specialist interest in online educational technology enhanced learning will need relevant information at an appropriate time. This could be provided at a school department or faculty level and this will have clear links to the staff online teaching development plan. Hence, online educational development strategy will influence any UK educational school technological improvement in the future.

(2) Environmental protection technological products to farmers‘ agricultural needs

Why do environment protection technological products are needed to be invent? Nowadays, global air and water pollution is serious. I shall indicate UK farmers why need to buy any high technological environment protection products. UK has many farming is polluted by the water and air pollution. It will influence UK farmers' income if whose farm land (natural resource) is polluted by water or air (natural resource). Even it will influence UK citizen will encounter food shortage if UK farmers can not grow any fresh and health food to provide the enough food numbers to eat every day. Moreover, air and water pollution will influence UK citizen drink the polluted water and breathe the dirty air to live every day. This natural resource (air and water challenge) will influence UK citizen health to cause illness , even death every easily. So, UK government can not neglect the natural environment pollution challenge. The environmental protection technology will help the UK and development countries to solve the challenge of climate change to avoid or reduce farming, foods, or vegetable or fruits or rice, pork, livestock numbers loss threats, i.e. the development and deployment of low carbon energy technology, including technology for the efficient use of energy. The commercialization of low carbon energy and energy efficiency technologies in the UK, with a specific focus on the demonstration and deployment phases of bringing low carbon technologies to UK market.

● Climate technology of global warming success to UK farmers

Climate alarmists were able to convince a large part of the Western public and a majority of Western politicians of the cause of fighting against the global warming. It supposes itself in an instinctive preference for collectivist solutions in economic and social spheres, with negative to disastrous consequences when scientists are applied in practice, so UK government needs to concern global warming challenge, due to it is possible that it will influence UK natural environment weather to be poor to influence many UK farmers' agricultural and vegetable and fruit and rice wheat etc. food growth successfully. What is the global warming influence to cause disease? For example, ecological alarmists and activists (eco-warriors) never admit they are wrong, they long pursued their fear mongering campaign against chlorine. Their success in branding DDT a dangerous substance had a negative impact on the malaria eradication campaign in poorer parts of the world. Alternatives to be have been far less effective and the result has been the resurgence of malaria cases and the manifold increase in malaria -caused deaths to the largest extent in Africa. The UK Government needs to deliver a low carbon economy and to meet UK ambitions emission reduction target. So, low carbon and environmental protection technology researching and development will reduce the carbon intensity of energy production as well as reduce energy demand, towards meeting the contributing UK's ambitions production as well as reduce energy demand, and renewable energy goals. The use of energy (including transportation fuel) and the UK's targets on climate change, for example, by helping the UK make a step change in increasing deployment of renewable energy, improving UK energy efficiency and helping low carbon technologies reach the market. The development of low carbon technologies, and to realize the benefits of doing so in terms ensuring security of energy supply for the UK future economy development.

In UK, private sector investment in technology innovation in the low carbon energy sector will other sectors of the economy. So, in UK energy technologies are likely needed to be developed to avoid dangerous climate change, or an acceptable cost. So, in the future, UK government will need to consider to research environment protection and low carbon energy technology. The activities will reduce carbon emissions, or have the potential to reduce carbon emissions on the longer term, through the use of energy technology will accelerate development and deployment of low-carbon energy and energy efficiency technologies will capacity in the demonstration and deployment of low carbon technologies. Innovation in the energy sector is the only way to identify, develop and reduce the costs of new and improved technologies for the extractions, generation, distribution and use of energy. It has long been an important means of achieving the UK's energy policy aims of a secure and affordable energy supply, as well as to develop the environmentally friendly technologies that are required in UK response to climate change, i.e. nuclear, wind or water, sun energy technology, which is future new energy technology is suitable to research to create to apply instead of current electricity energy.

How global warming influences UK agriculture growth. Scientists have also been fighting the use of chlorine in municipal water systems to kill various strands of bacteria. Chlorine reduces by about 80% the number of alimentary tract diseases relative to polluted, unchlorinated water. A relatively new genetically modified agricultural products. They were partly successful in Europe, such as UK (some countries banned genetically modified products) in spite of the fact that neither history nor research supports their case. People began to modify plants as early as the beginning of the agricultural revolution (8000 to 10,000 years ago), when they started seed selection and who have continued ever since. The green revolution of the 1960 year brought about strains of grans and rice more resistant to a variety of local conditions. The effects have been that countries like India, which had suffered from recurrent famines over the millennia, became self-sufficient in food due to the resultant sharp increase in agricultural productivity. It was a real science and technology over the poverty dominating most of human history. But it is precisely the products of science and technology that ecologists are so deathly afraid of. In an interesting study in a quarter (28%) of clinically analyzed cases of obsessive compulsive disorder were cases resulting from the fear of global warming. To destroy the modern, whether industrial or postindustrial, civilization, human have to destroy an important engine of economic growth, that is its energy sources. And this is what eco-warriors try to achieve under the banner of against global warming. Thus, UK government will have responsibility to attempt to research new technology to fight global warming challenge for itself farmer benefits and even global benefits both on the future. Hence, high technological environment protection products will be future developed and developing coutries‘ farmers needs.

- Agricultural development technology

Some economists indicate that there are five trends reshape to impact rural America' future economy. They include that digital economy will shift future America rural economy. US quality of life will change a lot, the US rural economy will stay uneven, US commodities will compete in global markets and will give less benefit to US rural economy and US new products will revolutionize US agriculture economy.

The first aspect impacts to US agriculture economy, the US future rural economy stays uneven. Growth will concentrate in 4 out of 10 rural places and they have scenery, a retail hub, or one next to a city in US. The impact on rural America includes some rural places will try to manage growth , but many places on a quest for new economic engines. Thus, it will bring these questions to US rural economy impact, such as : Who will be US businessmen clients? The struggling farmers? The struggling farm-dependent country? The booming mountain area? The rural area transforming into city?

The second aspect impacts to US agriculture economy, due to US commodities will compete in global markets if it will bring a smaller benefit in US rural economy. Then, US farm scale will cut costs and competition fewer US farms and places will depend on farm income. What is the impact of commoditization on rural America? There are more farms depend on area jobs and it creates a new imperative to add value. What is the impact of commodity on US clients? The need for competitive commodities remains, but the payoff for added value is rising and community impacts are important.

The third aspect impact to US agriculture economy, new products will revolutionize agriculture. Major, shift from commodities to products, spurred by biotech, means two agriculture in the future and two rural America . Hence, US future agriculture determination the rural economy will be declined. A future new US agriculture supply chain integrator will be caused from the traditional farming supply chain procedure the change to outsourced contractor farming supply chain procedure, such as: In beginning, from farmer will outsource supply chain contract to processor, then contract to distributor and contract to food retailer final step.

The fourth aspect impacts to US agriculture economy, what will be two agricultures impact to the US future economy? The first US agriculture impact will be US commodity agriculture. It focuses on production capabilities, farming foods production will be thin margins maintained with technology and big sale. The second US agriculture impact will be product agriculture. It focuses on consumer needs, farming foods production margins will be protected by capturing value and building business relationship. Thus, it will bring these questions concern what the impact of product agriculture which can influence to US economy. How to apply biotechnological agricultural techniques and farming product application to raise US farming productivity? How to build world class agricultural (farm) producing chains that benefit to US farming produces production method? How can US faming foods producers participation or lead in product chains?

In the fifth aspect impacts to US agricultural economy, it is digital economy impacts US rural agriculture. Future diversity economic base can encourage US farming product agriculture to enter rural digital agricultural service consumption sector to change US agricultural consumer individual shopping habit. What will impact to US farmers? Digital agricultural economy will bring these questions: Who will lead in broadband digital agricultural technology? How to launch e-markets and businesses and how to cooperate with US rural farmers? What will impact on US agricultural on natural resource management aspect and on how to US commodity to build amenity strategies? However, rural America's future will be shaped by policies that will encourage agricultural technology adoption, it will enhance farming worker skills, it will improve rural quality of life and it will ensure access to capital to bring US agricultural economy growth.

Considering a more growth accounting perceptive on productivity growth. According to the analysis in Fernald (2015) which uses a multi-sector growth model for the projections. It indicated that although, the details differ and if bases projections on TFP data since 2004, it also implies a preferred point estimate of 1.6% per year in US over this short period. The " fundamentals" of labor-productivity growth (namely, growth in total factor productivity , TFP) have exceeded the actual realization for reasons that reflect the unwinding of dynamic of labor quality and capital depending associated with the great recession. Thus, how to raise labor quality which concerns how to raise educational level to young people in any country will be one labor economic challenge in US in the future.

Fernald (2015) also explained " the shortfall" in productivity growth relative to fundamentals reflects, at least in part, the unwinding of two dynamics associated with the great recession. He indicated that first, at the end of the great recession business had a lot of capital relative to labor, which has attended the need of add capacity to meet demand in recent years. In contrast to the outsized growth in capital deepening from 2007 to 2010 year, we have seen capital "shallowing" since 2010 year. Second, businesses fired low-skilled workers during the recession, which raised labor quality in 2007 year to 2010 year period. As these potential workers have been rehired, the growth rate of labor quality has added less.

Thus, on the one hand, when one country encounters economic recession, many employers will like to employ high educational level and high skilled labor to raise productivity. If US encountered economic recession, but it had none (lacked) enough high educational level and high skilled knowledgeable workers to be supplied to the labor market in US. Then, US will encounter long term economic recession period, it can't shorten economic recession period. Thus, US will need to let many US young people have effort to study to prepare enough high educational level knowledge to do different kinds of professional or high knowledgeable or high technological jobs in future US labor market.

However, US high knowledgeable labor can also assist US businessmen to raise productivity growth. Due to labor quality could be grown by high educational and increasing number of knowledgeable workers. On the other hand, moreover, if there are many US young married parents who will either choose not born any babies for next generation or choose born only one to four children. Then, future US will have a small numbers of young people to be supplied to primary schools, high schools, even universities to study. It also means the university level graduate student numbers will decrease also. So, low birth rate factor can also influence the high knowledgeable labor numbers to be supplied to future US labor market.

So, I recommend that US government needs to encourage many young parents choose born next generation and provides student loans to lend to poor families to support whose children can have more chance to attempt to go to high schools or universities to study in the future.

(3) Environment protection and air and water pollution influence green gas man-made energy householder useful needs

Some future economists indicated reasons to explain why UK government and businessmen needed to consider how to develop natural environment protection technology to avoid global warming challenge to influence UK economy development. They indicated the anthropogenic (human-made) global warming resulting from the increase in "greenhouse gas". They offered their perspectives on the scientific valid of anthropogenic global warming phenomenon, its probability of occur and expected consequences and is dominated by technologists, economists and political scientists, who considered the need to make the horribly costly adjustments in energy generation and usage suggested by climate alarmists. Many stress that global warming is primarily caused by other phenomena than human use of fossil fuels or human activities in general. They are looking at the activities of the sun and impact of the larger universe as the main source of global warming and stress that global warmings (plural) happen intermittently with global cooling. I shall explain why global climate warming will influence to the political and economics of the issue to UK country. For it is the latter, rather than the global warming itself, that will pose a challenge to the Western world, such as UK and the world at large in the future. Scientists concerned who should move forward with policy measures to avert the alleged disaster. They also apply manufacturing theories to support enough to frighten politicians into action and scare societies into acceptance of measures that would sharply reduce UK citizen their living standards. Otherwise, UK politicians had support that bureaucracies were established, money allocated and lobbies created dependent on the new kind of subsidies. In consequences, climate alarmism and resultant interventions in national economies and human activities have become the increasingly wide spread and increasingly cost reality. With the growing availability of money distributed, and even more promised, a range of benefit of the global warming machinery has been on the increase. So, if UK government did not concern how to innovate new weather protection technology to avoid climate change adverse (poor) influence. It is possible that billions of dollars of UK public money are needed to spend on research global warming challenge because global warming will influence UK agricultural industry. UK agricultural industry is one important export income source to raise UK GDP income every year. If global warming become very serious to influence UK weather to be bad to cause UK farmers who can not grow good taste food and vegetable to supply to domestic and overseas food consumers to eat. Then, UK will loss much GDP income from local agricultural export sale. It seems global warming and agricultural production which has direct relationship to influence UK economy development in the future.

The main problem with climatology is that it must be based as already stressed on very many variables affecting climate and too few hard data necessity. Differences apply not only with respect to the scale of changes obtained, but even to their direction (rising or declining temperature). Some weather scientists indicated to concern global warming challenge. In consequence, it would be impossible to discover if and where errors were made not only in estimating relationships between variables but also in the quality of data used. (Hauser, J. Tellis, G. J; Griffin, A. 2006) They were comparing average temperatures measured some 30, 40 or 50 years ago by, say, 90 % weather stations in the countryside and 10 % stations in the cities with contemporary average temperatures measured by weather stations located today on 50:50 basis in the countryside and cities. Then, one could obtain the increasing temperatures without any real world climate or even weather changes. Comparability would be ensured if the same number of countryside-located and city-located weather stations had been compared for different periods. The alarmists intentionally mix up " temperature growth" with the trend of temperature growth. To give an example, if in the first decade the temperature grew by 0.5 % degree, in second decade it grew by 0.3 % and in third decade it grew by 0.1%, what was registered was a growth in the temperature, but certainly not a trend of growing temperature. A fourth decade should, on the basis of the trend, bring about no change in the temperature.

To conclude, scientists believed that global warming was caused by human's bad behavior more than natural environment influence. So, it is human's responsibility needs to solve this challenge, due to who feel earning profit aim is more important to protect natural environment, e.g. air and water pollution , due to manufacturing process is the main factor. So, UK has responsibility to attempt to research how to solve global warming challenge , such as it has many famous scientists who can devote their scientific skills to cooperate to solve global warming challenge with other countries' scientists. Some weather scientists also hypothesized that human may be at the end of the present warming period. If they are right, it would be bad for humanity, as warmer periods have always been associated with better conditions for economic activity. To sum up, scientists believed that global warming will influence human economic activity to be bad.

(4) Artificial intelligent automation products useful needs in robotics manufacturing industry

Nowadays, UK computer and space explore technology had reached the mature stage. It means that UK government ought not need to continue spend much resource to research these two kind technologies. Otherwise, the automatic manufacturing technology, e.g. human intelligence new product. It has need to develop because human intelligence machines will bring beneficial to satisfy human everyday life need, e.g. hospital patients' activities need, if the patent who can not walk easily, but the human intelligence machine can assist the patient walk to anywhere conveniently. So, he/she does not need to sit on wheel chair and apply the human intelligence machine man to help him/her to drive on the intelligence automatic driving vehicle to go to anywhere conveniently.

Otherwise, increased automation in low wage countries, e.g. China, Korea, Africa, Hong Kong etc. which have traditionally manufacturing firms, could use automatic technological manufacturing to bring lose cost advantage and potentially lose their ability of achieving rapid economy growth by shifting workers to factory jobs. So, UK government and businessmen needs to consider automation technology development, i.e. 3D printing manufacturing industry will encourage UK companies to move manufacturing process, closer to gain the biggest advantage from this 3D automation technology development.

A growing concern of premature de-industrialization in energy and developing countries could require new models and a need un-skillful the UK workforce. In the future, the best way toward for UK cities will reduce their exposure to automation is to boost their technological dynamic and attract more UK skilled workers. Automation technology progress can give UK manufacturers' employee benefits, such as long term healthy productivity improvement, raising productivity efficiency and product quality, macroeconomic and microeconomic effects of automation technological change, it's change will be beneficial to UK society, i.e.

automation active labor market policies, which could help UK job seekers find jobs from training to incentive to support self-employment to create high technological job employment chance in UK society. So, raising science, technology, engineering and math subjects update skills level are needed to UK any universities, which can be increasingly important in UK society, these factors could complicate the ability of UK high automation technology education to adopt to the UK automation manufacturing technological change. A talent mismatch already exists in UK, with many well UK educated workers can find employment in lower-skilled jobs.

Why are high automatic technology product development models needed to research to UK any manufacturers? UK government and manufacturers need to consider how to achieve high technology product development models. According to Hauser et al. (2006) indicated the high technology (high tech.) development process, is influenced by the innovative process, bringing products on exception value which stimulate product market demand. Innovation provides products the specific basis for which world economies compete with each other on the global market. Able to find new solutions, innovations generate significant changes in existing markets, destroy them, or create new marketing (Hauser et al. 2006). So, UK manufacturers need to concern on any manufacturing high technology product development process because which can influence any new products development to manufacture to sell to any overseas or domestic both markets successfully.

What is high tech. product meaning? Mohr et al. (2010) argues that there are two reasons why it is important to clarify and specific high technology : (1) due to the impact of technologies on the economy, attempts are made to classify economic production and incomes ; (2) due to the impact of high tech. on the environment. Standard marketing strategies are being modified and adopted , therefore, it is necessary to know the products to focus on. Why UK manufacturers need to consider high technological product process. Nowadays, high tech. products are complex, advanced, requiring specific technical knowledge, which is technologically not discontinued and being produced at the companies which have twice as many technical personnel and invest twice as many in scientific research and development than other companies. Moreover, these products are time-sensitive as scientists are continuously searching for new approaches for invention of more advanced technologies which make all preceding ones lower-ranking. The most important, nowadays global consumers will adopt the particular technology. It means that global customers may delay adopting new high-tech. products and in order to mitigate the prolonged uncertainty require a high degree of education and information about the product and need post-purchase reassurance.

Anyway, nowadays customer individual needs in high tech. environments are characterized by sudden changes related to unpredictable fashion. Even, consumers concern about how to preserve new product' competitive technological standard is completely incompatible with technological uncertainty. The most important factor is the prevalence rate of any new products development process, which is influenced by slower than of traditional products. In many cases high-tech. automatic product market are being materialized slower than which are expected. The technological uncertainty challenges will exist in development process, such as uncertainty related to the timetable for development of the question whether the new product will be function as promised. In automatic high-tech. industries, the time requires for product development is difficult to predict as , commonly, it takes longer than expected , uncertainty related to unanticipated consequences and uncertainty about the product life cycle related to competition products. In conclusion, these factors will influence new automatic technology product development process unsuccessful, so UK manufacturers will need to concern on any high technological automatic product's manufacturing process.

Before, all over the world presented picture of demonstrate in London on the occasion of the meeting of the G20. Some economists indicated disastrous economy consequences will occur to any one of Western country , such as UK, so if any one of Western country did not consider automatic technology development to itself country. They indicated one example, such as material incentives to produce disappeared throughout Russia and, when Society leadership called off the experiment, the country faced industrial output reduced to 10% of what had been registered in 1914 and agricultural output reduced to such low levels as to cause widespread famine.

Why would UK encounter disastrous economy consequences if UK government did not encourage manufacturers spend money to invest to innovate automatic technology industry? According to a variety of anthropological studies, a collectivity is unable to operate efficiently with everybody giving talent workers have chance to devote whose best effort to manufacture any high technological products, e.g. human intelligence vehicle or airplane. Hence, economic incentives are needed to UK manufacturers to invest high technological automatic industry development. Because the economists predict UK will have many talent worker numbers, their number will be more than a certain number of normal effort workers, due to UK technological education level is very excellent to provide to train many young technological manufacturing students to find this kind of high technological manufacturing job. So, the high technological manufacturing job seekers will increase and it won't decrease to UK job market in the future.

Assuming that UK high technological automatic manufacturing workers who would desire only to introduce changes in the workings of the international economic order and policies of countries participating in the present economic order rather than change the order itself, what will be UK manufacturers their specific economic preferences in the future? It implies tnat either concentrate on spending more investment to automatic high technological development, e.g. human intelligence automatic high technological products or still concentrate on spending more investment to common traditional technological products.

However, UK was a developed Western country which had had strong automatic high technological development effort very long time. Otherwise, it compared to some developing countries, such as Asian China, Hong Kong, Korea etc. Asian countries their future economic growth rate will show un- surprising , different patterns, so the Asian countries has weak effort to invest high automatic technological product development, such as human intelligence technological development. The catching-up process suggests low economic growth rate in the high automatic technological product development to the Asian developing countries in the future.

Hence, the future economists predict that it views as probable successors of the Western world economic leadership if any Western country , such as UK manufacturers who prefer to invest to any high automatic technological products development , e.g. developing on human intelligence automatic technological products more than traditional common technological products development. On the one side, but it seems important to stress that two very poor countries among the challengers-China and India-are examples of countries that changed their institutions and economic policies from no or little economic freedom to more economic freedom. Because there two countries whose governments prefer to lend loans to encourage their country manufacturers prefer to invest high automatic technological products manufacturing. On the other side, attitudes toward foreign direct investment (FDI) have undergone change since the 1960 s and a large majority of less developed countries, e.g. China and India are now competing strongly among themselves and with developed market economies for direct investment from multinational companies. So, UK will face China and India high automatic technological product competitors in the future. And in fact, all countries that joined Western developed economies did that without much (if any) external inflow of public resources. It is right time that UK government needs to lend loans to encourage domestic manufacturers to invest high automatic technological products to raise whose international high technological products sale effort to win its future competitors. So, machine resources will be increased demand to o UK manufacturers if who chose to spend machine resources to innovate to manufacture any new and high technological automatic products to raise human daily life needs in thc future. It means that it is right time UK manufacturers need buy much machines to prepare to manufacture many future high technological automatic products when these machine prices are low. Because the future global machine prices will possible be raised if many China and India manufacturers will also buy many machines in the future. For example, USA government had provided much financial support to assist sugar cane producers to develop their businesses. And they are dependent to a much larger extent than sugar cane producers and sugar processors in the USA on government. Without very high subsidies to renewable energy generation, they would not have survived at all. So, USA government had been the first country which could lent much financial assistance to encourage domestic renewable energy generation manufacturers to develop high technological energy manufacturing business. So, UK government needs follow USA to lend financial assistance to encourage domestic high technological automatic industry development. Future economists also predict China and India will be competitors for future leadership in the global economy, special high technological products. China has been the media and analyst's favorite for quite some time. Quantitative projections have seemingly supported such expectation. Such as China and India had manufactured many high technological new space rockets products, ocean war large ships etc. Moreover, China has become one of the major world trade players in the early twenty-first century.

Many long-term forecasts, assuming similarly high economic growth rates in the decades ahead, predict that China will surpass the USA in terms of aggregate GDP somewhere between 2020 and 2030 or later, say between 2030 and 2050 year. The future economists conclude on the basis of these predictions that China will not only pass the USA in aggregate product (GDP), but its economy and economic policies will influence the rest of the world to a similar extent that the USA does at present.

I stressed a very important point, namely that the UK future high technological automatic product competitor China and India, namely that economies not only grow, but in the process change their structure. China and India have been industry very rapidly (the first transition) and building the physical infrastructure that accompanies industrialization changes to technology in the future. However, at a certain per capita GNP level the two countries, such as China and India will face another structural shift when which technological development will reach the mature stage in the future. China and India had been primarily historical pattern of economic development because the shift in the role of engine of growth from industry to services is to a much greater extent a qualitative shift. Both higher and different skills are required. And, even more importantly, interactions generating ideas driving the highly human-capital-intensive service economy require a much freer environment, not only in the economic area. Chinese exports have been heavily labor-intensive. This being the case, they contributed to the expansion of industrial employment, offering for the first time in the history of China a taste of (very modest) prosperity to more than 100 million new industrial workers and their families. This is the major component of the success accomplished by Chinese economic growth. Richer trade partners create room for more trade, so the Chinese should hope that intra-South trade, that is, trade between the emerging economies of Asia, the Middle East, Africa and Latin America, will open up new and growing opportunities. I presume that if Western economy , such as UK did not developed high technological automatic industry to stable their social welfare, so thoroughly slowed down their economic growth.

Will it allow China to accomplish the transition to a mature, innovation, service sector-based market economy? It has allowed the economy to industrialize much more successfully, even it the labor shift from agriculture to industry has not yet been completed. But it is a long way off the next major test: the second high technological industry transition of the economic structure to China. Bear in mind that Russia attempted it twice and failed at both attempts.

But even, assuming that China at some point in the future does succeed in accomplishing the second transition, will it be able to supersede the USA, for example, as the main global high automatic technological innovation center if it wants to become the No.1 global high technological industry economy? Given the nature of the centralized state and its stability to collect financial resources , China's ability to increase research and development expenditure to high automatic technological products and to hire a mass of researchers, engineers, technicians and other specialists should not be doubted. This process in already taking place.

But , again, Soviet Russia already exceed the USA in the R&D/GDP ratio in the 1970s, long before the communist collapse, with no effects on its innovativeness. Inputs matter less than outputs, quantity in the innovation process mean much less than quality. The latter characteristics depends importantly on economic, civic and even political institutions. Otherwise, independent India had three options open to it in 1946s. It could pursue spontaneous economic development, with some state intervention to be sure, along the lines of basically free market capitalism; it could turn the clock back and try to recreate the rural-agricultural and handicraft based. The dominant way of thinking was Society -style priority to industrialization and , within industralization , priority to heavy industry. In other words, not textiles and clothing, which has been developing well in India since the mid- nine teen century, but production of sewing machines and , even better, production of machines the produce sewing machines.

The results were only to be expected. The heavy stress on the expansion of capital-intensive heavy industries in a very poor country quickly strained the ability of the Indian economy to generate adequate savings. Moreover, some of these industries were above the level of industrial competence of an underdeveloped economy. Thus, the amount of required resources (capital, skilled labor) was usually larger per unit of output than in the same industries in more mature, richer industries economies. In another view point, India will develop light industries, just as any other poor country with a great deal of unskilled labor, had a comparative advantage and no less importantly, an economy in which, due to their low capital/labor ratio, light industries could employ many more people, spreading prosperity more widely in a poor country. So, it explain that why China will have more effort to develop heavy high technological industry in the future. Thus, India got less economic efficiency, less employment than in a spontaneously developing economy, less ability to compete internationally in light industries suitable for an underdeveloped economy and finally got heavy industry unable to compete even on the domestic market and, therefore requiring no less heavy a dose of protection. Overall India got an underperforming economy, in particular in its relations with the rest of the world.

To conclude by comparing the performance of the traditional sectors of the Indian economy and the performance of its modern, human -capital-intensive subsector of manufacturing and skill intensive service sector. The latter both employ workers with high-and medium -high skillful level (in branches ranging from computer software and biotechnology and pharmaceutical high technological light industry). India is ahead of China in terms of the output and export of such products and services. Thus, it implies that UK ought concentrate on developing high automatic heavy high technological industry, e.g. human intelligence technological products because these industry is not better development to other many countries' strong effort , such China and India large population countries.

- US artificial intelligent robotic manufacturing factory needs

In the past, there fundamental forces have shaped US work labor market, includes an increase in the returns to education. General education upgrading and the large numbers of female need to work. How educational attainment, demographics and human capital will be predicted to influence US future labor market. Some economists believe education is useful to influence US future labor market. They indicate the social returns to education policies today depend on the relative prices that labor of different educational levels will command in future US labor market; current US labor market trends appear to leave a large group behind; less educated males. The rationale for social policies target specifically to this population is strengthened if predicted future outcomes in US labor market will lead this less educated male group numbers to fall down.

How to supply educational level components to influence future changes in US labor supplied? It can change in the size of the US working age population, it can change in hours worked conditional on being of working age, and it can change in the skills (effective human capital units) to US workers of different education levels, gender and age . In US , the labor is supplied by both highly educated men and women increased substantially relative to the supply of labor by the less educated. Among US males this is largely , due to an increase in educational attainment; highly educated

US males did not differentially increase their supplied compared to less educated males nor did their experience differential increases in their human capital policy in US. For US females, some economists found large increases in the labor supplied by US working age women that are due to both large increases in hours worked and increase in educational attainment. So, I assume that future US will have many high educational level female labors to work in US society.

Today, human history is at the beginning of a growth industrial revolution. Developments in genetics, artificial intelligence, robotics, nanotechnology, 3D printing and biotechnology will be popular to influence US future job market change. For example, smart systems, product-homes, factories, farms or cities with help to solve problems ranging from supply chain management to climate change. The rise of the sharing economy will allow US human to monetize everything from their empty house to their car.

Due to the future patterns of consumption will change to trend high technology life enjoyment, it will cause production and employment will also change to employ high technological production labor. As entire industries adjust, most US occupations are changed to high technological manufacturing industries. When some US jobs are threatened by others grow through a change in the skill sets required to do them. a key element in understanding how the benefits and burdens of the growth.

Nowadays, the current technological changes of humans and machines , but rather an opportunity for work to truly become a channel though which human recognize full potential. As US is a high technological developed country. I assume many US employers will choose to act to be the first high technological and invention manufacturing leader to encourage which labors need to learn high technological production methods to prepare manufacture any new technological products to sell in the future US domestic or foreign both markets. Thus, it is possible that future high technological manufacturing labor numbers will be shared large go e.g. 50 to 60% future total US labor market.

How can future US labor market affect job creation and productivity growth? US future economic growth requires factor reallocation across US firms and continuous replacement of technologies. US labor market influences US economy dynamism by their impact on the supply of a key factor, skilled workers to US new and expanding firms, US growth -favoring labor market includes portable pension plans and health insurance united to the current US employers, individualized wage-setting and US public income insurance systems that encourage mobility and risk taking.

US future economic growth arises as production shifts from less to more successful firms though the reallocation of factors of production . US labor market can advance restructuring. Overly regulations tend to create a system in which a large share of economic activity occurs in US small firms without the ability to grow. US labor market should be organized to promote potential high growth US firms, especially through decentralized and individualized wage setting, portable jobs.

In the future, US will have many key importance of high growth firms. US capitalism entails a process of creative destination. New ideas continuously challenges act structures, giving rise to structural transformation as successful innovations and new products firms and industries will arise and obsolete ones will decline in US society.

Martin , J. P. (2012) studies pointed to high-growth forms (sometimes known as gazelles) as the main drivers of this process. In the US , an estimated 1% of firms creation 40% of all new jobs and 5% create almost 70% of new jobs. A review of the studies of US firms growth reveals some common findings . US high-growth firms are crucial to net job growth, generating a large share of all net jobs . This is particularly pronounced in recessions, when US high-growth firms continue to grow when other US firms deadline. US small firms are over-represented among high-growth firms, but these US firms come in all sizes . A small subgroup of large high growth firms are major job creators. Such as US high -growth firms are younger on average, US young and small high high-growth firms grows, not through mergers and acquisition and make a larger contribution to net employment growth than do US larger and older higher growth firms, high growth firms are present in all industries. Through they are slightly overrepresented in service industries in US.

Some economists predict that future US will be a flexible labor market, the marginal product of labor and the average wage in an industry should tend toward equally across US firms. Taking advantage of a legislative change to raise cost to US employers a study measured the gap between the marginal product of labor and the average wage in an industry before and after the reform. The gap increased after the legislation, which suggests that the legislation reduced allocative efficiency. Their studies have suggested that total factor productivity could increase by as much as 30% in China and India of they were to attain the US level of allocative efficiency across firms within individual industries. The result implies that plants with low total factor productivity are too large and plant with high total factor productivity are too small relative to the US benchmark of allocative efficiency.

What is allocative efficiency meaning? It occurs when the mix of product produced matches consumer preferences (where marginal benefit equals marginal cost). There products and services are the most profitable, thereby promoting economic growth other research also indicate a strong quantitative effects of strict employment protection legislation on the rate of reallocation in US industries experiments. By relaxing employment protection rules to US developed countries, such as UK, UK etc. with the strictest legislation could increases their reallocation rate by an estimated 50% in the most dynamic sectors, those that benefit most from flexibility.

The effect appears to be particularly strong on the entry-exist margin, which is arguably, especially importation for creative destruction. In future US, if manufacturing industry can have high technological production method to achieve reallocation rate to efficiency to every manufacturing industry. It can have benefit to economic growth, due manufacturing process can be move efficient to avoid cost. Also high technological manufacturing reallocation rate innovation method can influence the future US number of jobs lost in contracting or existing US firms as well as the number of jobs gained in new or expanding US firms in future a certain period divided by the average number of existing jobs. So, US high technological manufacturing reallocation rate innovation method will bring disadvantages to cause many contracting or existing firms job lost, but it will also increase the number of jobs gained in new or expanding firms in US. Thus, if future US manufacturing industry can have high technological reallocation rate innovated successfully. It will raise many new job chances in new or expanding firms in US, but it also have chance to cause many contracting or existing firms job lost or the same time.

What will expected to impact of future computerization on US labor market outcomes? Some economists estimated, about 47% of total US employment is at risk, due to that US wages and educational attainment will exhibit a strong negative relationship with an occupation's probability of computerization. They indicated that the poor performance of global labor markets across advanced economies has intensified the debate about technological unemployment among economists more recently. Indeed, over the past, decades, computers have substituted for a number of jobs, including the functions of bookkeepers, cashier and telephone operators (

Bresnahan, 1999, MGI, 2013).

Although the extent of these developments remains to be seen, estimates by MGI (2013) suggests that sophisticated algorithms could substitute for approximately 140 million full time knowledge workers world wise. Hence, when technological process throughout economic history has largely been confined to the machine of manual tasks, requiring physical labor, technological progress in the twenty-first century can be expected to contribute to a wide range of cognitive tasks, which until have largely remained a human domain. Of course, may occupations being affected by these developments act still far from fully computerization, meaning that the computerization of some tasks will simply free-up time for human labor to perform other tasks. Nonetheless, the trend is clear: computers increasingly challenge human labor in a wide range cognitive tasks (Brynjolfsson and Mc Afee, 2011).

Thus, it seems that future US computerization job trend will influence some US traditional labor hand made manufacturing industry to divide some part job duty to let computerization work. However, it will not cause many US manufacturing labor to be dismissed. It can still keep some US manufacturing labors to US employers' needs in the future.

- Genetics, human intelligence, robotics, nanotechnology, 3D printing and biotechnology technological industry development

In future our high technological product enjoyment need, these kinds of jobs will be needed to increase development in genetics, human intelligence, robotics, nanotechnology, 3D printing and biotechnology. For example, smart systems homes, factories, farms grids or cities will help tackle problems ranging from supply chain management to climate change. The rise of US economy growth will allow US people to monetize everything from their empty house to their car in US. These new technological products development will change US patterns of consumption, production and employment adaption are also be changed by US corporations, US government and individuals.

Why will the technological revolution be broader socio-economic, geopolitical and demographic drivers of change to influence future US social economic and consumption pattern change? Future US most occupations will also be changed. When some traditional old jobs are threatened by redundancy and other new technological jobs will grow rapidly, existing jobs are also changed in the skill sets required to do them. The debate is between some economists foresee limitless new job opportunities and foresee massive dislocation of US jobs. In fact, the reality is highly specific to future US high technological production industry, region and high technological occupation in question as well as how US production workers can be raised themselves ability to actions the upgrade level of high technological production ability from various stakeholders to manage high technological production method change.

Overall, this is a modestly positive outlook of US high technological production employment across future most high technological production industries with jobs growth expected in several sectors. However, it is also clear that this need for more talent in certain job categories is accompanied by high skills instability across all job categories. Combined together, future US net job growth and skills instability result in most US businesses with face major recruitment challenges and talent shortages, a pattern already evident in the result and set to get worse over next five years in possible. The question is how US businesses, government and individuals will react to these new technological job changes, due to talent shortage, mass unemployment and growing inequality challenges will encounter in future US society.

The current technological revolution does not need become a race between humans and machines , but rather an opportunity for work to truly become a channel through which US people recognize their potential. So, if US traditional low manufacturing skillful workers lack talent to learn new skills to prepare to do future new technological manufacturing jobs, such as 3 D printing, robotics, nanotechnology, biotechnological high technological products manufacturing jobs. Then, it will cause increasing of unemployment rate to some not talent US low manufacturing skillful workers. So, US government or high technological product industry employers need to consider this future unemployment challenge will be caused by high technological products manufacturing changing influences. It seems high technological development will cause these low manufacturing skillful workers unemployed rising numbers as well as high manufacturing skillful workers human capital shortage global challenges will exist.

In the future, the driver of changes to influence US demographic and socio-economic growth. They may include: changing work environments and flexible working arrangements. It means new technologies are enabling workplace innovations , such as remote working, co-working spaces and teleconferencing. Rising of the middle class in Asia markets. It means the world's economic center is shifting towards the Asia developing countries. Some economists predict that Asia will be projected to account for 66% of the global middle class and for 59% of middle class consumption by 2030 year. In addition, climate change, natural resource will be constraints to a greener economy. It means that climate change is a major driver of innovation as organizations search for measures to help adjust to its effects. As global economic growth consumers are needed to lead to demand for natural resources and raw materials, over explanation implies higher extraction most and degradation ecosystem and these challenges will also impact US employment changes needs. All US government also needs to concern future global economic change influence.

(5) Ecommerce information technological online trading development What are the four big factors of intangible assets? Some economists indicated they include knowledgeable capital, human capital, social capital and entrepreneurs capital. Nowadays, globalization and increased competition will cause new types of pressure to influence US economic growth. So, US companies need have flexibility, the ability to immediately adapt to market developments, and pro-activism in creating future markets. The relative importance of physical growth: However, soft production factors, that is those related to personal knowledge are becoming more important to influence US future economic growth, which regards to human capital and knowledge as driving factor of economic growth in industries developed countries, such as US.

All these soft production factors can be grouped in what is known intangible assets. These assets can be defined as non-material factors that contribute to enterprise performance in the production of products or the provision of services, or that are expected to generate future economic benefits to the entities or individuals that control their deployment (Akerlof & Kranton , 2000).

Ecommerce trading method information technological shopping model owns intangible asset, intangible asset website is such as tangible asset store to every online merchant as well as ecommerce soft production factors, such as website design is same to traditional business production factors to store, such as salespeople, land, store. So, ecommerce owns soft production factors and intangible asset comparative advantage to reduce cost in economic view to compare traditional store visiting purchase and sale model. Some economists had researched to have more reliable quantitative statistical information to do report in above four big factors how to effect on US regional economical growth influence. Their report indicated that returns from human and social capital are taken as homogeneous for US all regions. They also indicated these two sets of questions in their report. The first one, dealing with knowledge accumulation, addresses, among others the following issues:

(a) How does innovation and knowledge accumulation occur within firms and hoe does it impact on economic performance?

(b) What is the role of universities in regional, national and global knowledge accumulation processes?

The second set of questions addresses the key knowledge diffuses over space and how this diffusion impacts on economic performances.

In particular:

(c) To what extent knowledge diffusion is conditioned by spatial proximity?

(d) What is the impact of knowledge accumulation and diffusion on economic performance?

They indicated to answer these questions, having reliable measures of how innovation process occurs, of the actors that take part in it and the mechanisms that are in place is important. They pointed out that the systemic nature of US regional intangible asset demands indicators that grasp two kinds of capabilities: network capabilities , i.e. connectivity, both intra-and-inter-regional and organizational capabilities, as well as their dynamic in US. These indicators have been applied to the study of linkages and relationships between US firms and between US firms and US universities, highlighting the mechanisms through which those actors contribute to the processes of knowledge accumulation, generation and diffusion.

They also found results: How does knowledge accumulation occur within US firms and how does it impact on US economic performance? They included collaborations with competitors are most commonly undertaken at early stages of the development projects, those with buyers and suppliers are more likely to result in the introduction of new products and processes: At the same, it has been highlighted that, regardless of the industry, the most innovative firms, i.e. those more able to absorb knowledge are more likely to participate in collaborative networks.

Thus, US future entrepreneurships need to offer knowledge accumulation opportunities for US regional firms and research institutions to benefit and contribute to global network of US expects to achieve rapid regional economic growth. US's entrepreneurships also needs to explore organizational innovation, those US firms whose structure enables learning by doing, using and interacting by relying, among other things on parallel development teams. Semi-autonomous work teams and reduced management layers are more likely to introduce new products to the future US domestic and foreign both markets.

What is the role of US universities in US regional, national and global knowledge accumulation processes? US universities can heavily influence US regional, national and global knowledge accumulation processes. For instance, when collaborating with multi-national enterprises, they may affect simultaneously the three level. Their report had highlighted interesting results on the local impact of universities: when it has been found that top ranked departments are significantly associated with partnerships involving spatially close industry partners, it has also emerge geographical proximity, is nt the main driver of collaboration choices. These are found to depend largely on US firms' networks and universities' specific characteristics. Among other things, the cultural traditional of academic institution has been shown to influence the ability to collaborate with industry and commerce research.

Networks characteristics have emerged as crucial in determining academic knowledge transfer: the better the access to international networks, the higher the patenting activity, have the knowledge transfer to any traditional service industries. This implies that the set of tools of knowledge based economic development should include not only research and development, but also clever ways of supporting academic research network. On conclusion, information technological ecommerce can assist economic growth more easy to compare traditonal visiting store business model, e.g. ebook, e-air ticket, ehotel room ticket, e-song, e-movie etc. information technological service or e-products had been accepted in popular to replace traditional paper book reading, paper air ticket, hotel room booking, watching movie and listening music etc. entertainment services. Hence, future information technology can be applied to electronic service consumption and entertainment model when any online consumers can use their service from internet conveniently.

Reference

Hauser, J. Tellis, G. J; Griffin, A. 2006. Research On Innovation: A Review And Agenda For Marketing Science. 25(6): 687-717.

Mohr, G. J. Griffin, A. 2010. Research On Innovation : A Review And

Agenda For Marketing Science. 25 (6): 687-717.

CHAPTER SEVEN

Online movie and television broadcasting industry impacts audience behavior

● ONLINE TELEVISION BROADCASTING CHARACTERISTICS

The television and broadcasting sector has been undergoing significant technological and structural changes, which have given consumers access to a great variety of communications and media services. Convergence is changing the way in which consumers use communication services and consume content, as it is available on new platforms and on various wireless portable devices. At the same time, technological change has impacted on regulation and conditions of competition. The penetration of new technologies and the dynamic effects of convergence are changing the way that consumers access and view audio visual content . Nowadays, it can be provided via multiple platforms: analogue or digital terrestrial broadcasts, satellite, cable or Internet Protocol (IP) and Over-the-Top (OTT) television.

A fundamental change affecting traditional broadcasting stems from the migration of networks to IP data transmission. Combined with significant broadband penetration, increases in bandwidth and the proliferation of digital devices, this has enabled different devices to use the same networks and has facilitated the ability of the communication industry to offer new and bundled services. This allows consumers to receive and decode video services across a variety of fixed and mobile devices. Technological developments affect the conditions of competition as they alter: the range and quality of services; the underlying costs; the extent of barriers to entry (new technologies provide new means by which the market is contested);

the ability of customers to switch suppliers; and pricing mechanisms (technological developments allow for provision of pay per view services). Therefore, digitisation generally reduces barriers to entry.

While technological evolution and the emergence of new products and services have rendered visual media markets more competitive, some developments in the television and broadcasting market create challenges for competition policy. Product market definition in television and broadcasting has become a serious challenge due to technological changes and convergence. To properly define the relevant market, for example, US NCAs news must have a clear understanding of demand and supply side substitutions along the entire value chain. The market analysis must also take into account the different variables specific to audiovisual products and service markets, like high fixed costs, low marginal costs, bundling, non-price competition, two-sided or multi-sided nature of markets, vertical integration or rapid technological development. Convergence has led to situations of triple play, with telecommunications, cable TV and the Internet, or even quadruple play, with telecommunications, cable TV, Internet and mobile industry. Although market definitions will likely differ across jurisdictions and among individual markets, on a general level a wholesale market for content, a wholesale access market to the infrastructure and a retail market can be identified. A narrower market definition can be based on the type of: broadcaster, platform, pay TV services or premium content. Historically, different types of media (TV, radio, Internet or press) were viewed as separate product markets, but convergence has forced a number of NCAs to adopt a broader market definition (e.g. CME/Balkan News Corporation and TV Europe in Bulgaria). Similarly, representatives of the industry favour the adoption of a more inclusive product market definition. Even though convergence and technological changes have lowered barriers to entry, there are still significant challenges that may restrict market access. The doctrine gives a non-exhaustive list of examples: governmental policy, the presence of dominan.

Access to premium content is a serious bottleneck and a source of market power. In particular, premium sport events (e.g. Olympic Games or football matches) and new releases of movies, which have no substitutes, are essential to the successful functioning of pay TV providers. Barriers to accessing content can arise from the integration of content owners and broadcasters, exclusive contractual arrangements or from vertical foreclosures by a dominant firm. Premium content may also have an impact on competition in other non-TV markets. For instance, in triple or quadruple play markets, content can increase the attractiveness of the package. Market structure analysis is essential for US NCAs news to address challenges relating to access to content. A key issue is that a downstream broadcasting service provider may be able to leverage its market position to gain power in an upstream market for content. This upstream buyer's power would enable the exercise of additional market power in the downstream market.

In the scenario of a competitive downstream market, the structure of the upstream market has an important impact on market outcomes. NCAs may be most concerned when a merger between a downstream broadcaster and a provider of premium content threatens the availability of that content to competing broadcasters. This depends on the elasticity of supply of competing content. The analysis undertaken by Professor Fels shows that competition concerns in content markets cannot be ruled out, but any assessment of the likelihood of those issues arising depends on a complex, and often counterintuitive, analysis of market structure and conduct in both the upstream and downstream market. Moreover, the exclusive content strategy can lead to its fragmentation across platforms. To address this problem, some countries (e.g. Singapore) have imposed on subscription TV licensees a statutory obligation to cross-carry the exclusive content on the other subscription TV licensee's platform in its entirety and in an unmodified and unedited form. Specific challenges can be also identified for acquiring content by non-linear TV services (e.g. CanalSat/TPS in France). Finally, in some countries (e.g. Egypt) piracy has decreased the value of the premium content.

The broadcasting landscape all over the world has been undergoing significant technological and structural changes. These transformations have given consumers access to a greater variety of communications and media services than ever before. For example, in the past television content could be accessed by the viewer at a specific point in time and only at a fixed location. However, convergence is changing the way in which consumers use communications services and consume content as broadcasting content is increasingly available over the Internet and on various wireless portable devices. While the technological evolution and the emergence of new products and services have rendered media markets more competitive overall, thereby directly benefitting consumers, some market developments raise competition problems, especially in the area related to content.

Accordingly, the purpose of this Background Note is to examine competition issues that arise in the provision of television broadcasting to viewers and the extent to which these changes are making television broadcasting more competitive between online (computer or mobile electronic platform tool) and offline traditional television broadcasting entertainment platform channels. The topic is of timely importance from the perspective of the Global Competition Forum as broadcasting, both through radio and television services, forms an important part of the information and communications technologies (ICTs) and ensuring widespread access to broadcasting services may not only reduce the digital divide, but it may also help foster development and alleviate poverty. Ensuring widespread access to radio and television broadcasting is important for a number of economic and non-economic reasons both in the OECD as well as in non-OECD economies. Economically speaking, broadcasting is a significant economic sector in its own, and it can produce significant spill-over benefits in many related markets. Moreover, while radio and television broadcasting continues to be the major source of information in general, it constitutes "a principal source of information for illiterate segments of the population", which becomes particularly important in times of emergencies. Although the broadcasting sector has undoubtedly become more competitive in the future, competition authorities throughout the globe have become more active in launching policy interventions. In some cases these also involved a consideration of public interest criteria other than competition concerns. Social and cultural objectives pursued by regulatory policy in the broadcasting sector generally fall beyond the scope of this paper. However, it must be borne in mind that economic and non-economic objectives whether the television entertaiment program markers how deign their boradcasting programs can adapt to any online and offline television auidences , it means that they can accept to watch their television broadcasting entetainment program from any where when they apply mobile or computer platform to still feel enjoyable to watch their television entertainment programs, and with one intervention the authorities may simultaneously pursue both goals.

Today, it is clear that the disruptive potential from convergence is being realised in the broadcasting industry and as such the industry cannot easily be defined according to discrete characteristics of transmission, audience or even modes of viewing. If the television entertainment broadcasting program designer or decison maker still hopes to achieve the overall audiences number increases in the offline and online broadcasting market. As a consequence, many of the traditional rationales for broadcasting regulation have been removed and new competition concerns have arisen. Fundamental changes have occurred through a realignment of the boundaries between telecommunications and broadcasting sectors. These include:

• fixed and mobile broadband networks that are capable of carrying a diversity of voice and video content; • the internet that has blurred the distinction between private (telecoms) and public (broadcasting) communications; • distinctions between the character of the message whether data, voice, or audio visual images are obsolete, and • the equipment used to record, transmit and or receive messages is no longer relevant in distinguishing telecoms and broadcasting services.

● TV Online Threatens Traditional reasons

Online streaming of television has become the new "thing" of today. It is through the many outlets of watching shows online that many are able to accomplish making television the center of their daily-lives. Many of the most popular outlets include that of Hulu, Amazon Prime, and the most popular Netflix. Through these streaming services, people took TV watching to a whole other level. In fact it is in these archives that one can finish an entire series that are available. In order to do this many take the full advantage of using the mobile apps that come along with these sites. Using these sites individuals have been able to take their TV watching on the go with them in almost every place possible with Wi-Fi connection.

Who is watching more online television? The answer is pretty obvious; it is no surprise that younger people are the ones watching online streaming of television. For the generation where technology is readily available, it is no surprise that we turn to computers for our television time. In fact, it is because of this that those over at MarketingCharts were able to make their deductions that, "Yes, youth as a whole are watching less TV – and the decline appears to be accelerating."

According to MarketingCharts, between 2014 and 2015 the viewing between ages of 18-24 showed a decline from the previous years. One could then make the deduction that in the many of the shows that were watched during traditional television showings now are more likely to be watched streaming online.Thus far it is hard to predict how long online streaming of television will last. Could we see ourselves slowly become a generation solely dependent on the internet and separated from the television? Will popular networks now begin to cater to the online streamer? What is the fate of traditional television? Will it continue to remain relevant or will it eventually fade with time and history?

● What is online broadcasting attractive strengths? The Internet as the Anti-Television: Distribution Infrastructure as Culture and Power

Distribution asks us to revisit a classic question of media studies: How does the medium affect the content? Available computer and mobile watching sceen platform will replace traditional televison screen platform , which will demonstrate that the Internet was originally conceived of as the opposite of television: the anti-television. Over the course of several decades, however, the Internet was technologically retrofitted and transformed to make video distribution possible. Embedded in this transformation were competing ideas about what content and which audiences are valuable, and indeed how culture itself ought to work. The selection of videos available on the Internet today—and how that video looks—result from purposeful decisions made by actors who hoped that either the model of television or the Internet as anti-television would prevail.

Technically speaking, television and Internet traffic were at first like oil and water: fundamentally unmixable. The Internet was envisioned as a "point-to-point" network, meaning a system designed to facilitate communication between two nodes. Although some functionality in the Internet protocols allows the broadcast of data to all nearby nodes, uses like broadcasting to a large audience were never envisioned by the engineers who built the system. At the time computers were not capable of receiving or displaying video at all.

In communication network design, the distinction between point-to-point and broadcast systems is one of the most basic. The metaphor used to explain the point-to-point Internet given by engineer and Internet pioneer Vint Cerf is that of the postal network, with packets of data functioning like postcards. This is an apt metaphor that highlights the difference between broadcast and point-to-point. In over-the-air television broadcasting, a fundamental feature of the electromagnetic wave that radiates from a television station's transmission tower is that it makes no difference to the wireless signal whether it is received by one person or one hundred. Indeed, the cost of sending it—the cost of transmission—is the same in either case. Delivering television via satellite or via a cable network also employs a broadcast architecture and realizes the same benefit. In contrast, the costs of transmission of a postcard (and the Internet) scale linearly: in the case of one vs. one hundred recipients, 99 more postcards must be printed by the sender and 99 more postcards must be delivered by the mail carrier. Mail carriers must do 99 times more work, but television antennas need change nothing. 99 more postcards require 99 more stamps. In other words, unlike television broadcasting, the cost of transmission rises as the number of postcards transmitted increases.

The Internet could certainly have been designed differently, but a postcard-like system conformed with the design goals of early Internet engineers. When I click on a link or type in a Web address to read a news story published by The New York Times at nytimes.com, a reasonable person might assume that the information comes from New York City, from a computer owned by The New York Times. Thus, many audiences like to watch news from online channel more than traditional offline television channel. It is possible that many working people who need to watch news when they are catching public transportation tools to go back homes. So, online watching channel has more attractive strengths to persuade many news audiences to apply mobile or laptop electronic tools to watch news when they leaves their homes ever day.

So, due to convenient mobile or laptop carring watcing screen platform, audiences can download any past television entetainment broadcasting programs to watch from internet, no download fee charge, audiences can watch anywhere factors, they can influences many traditional television audiences choose to change visual watching channel from online channel. Then, traditional television broadcasting will encounter unpredictable broadcasting competitive market in global broadcasting industry.

- Online and offline entertainment broadcasting strategic thinking

Strategic thinking is often talked about as a management process, but it is not. So , often defined and even has frequently explored similar in many ways to ideas , such as " innovative thinking", leading , or " transformational changes". It is more often than not unclear what it is actually about.

For Googling online advertisement and social media business example, its " strategic thinking" brings up a lot of more general material on strategic management, but this tends to be think with concepts and theory, but thin or cognitive processes. Essentially, therefore, to understand strategic thinking one needs to have some understanding of the practical aspects of psychology.

Why does television broadcasting business needs to gather data from audience market? Because online television broadcasting is popular to attractive audiences to choose to apply mobile or laptop or desktop tools to watch any entertainment broadcasting programs from online website channel more than traditional offline television channel. So, the traditional offline television watching channel will be replaced by online entertainment broadcasting channel, if the traditional entertainment broadcasting program makers still hope to attract any young or old auidences to watch any broadcasting entertainment programs from television channel. They must need to gather data from television audiences market to compare what their entertainment broadcasting programs' strengths and weaknesses are: For example, some data input for potential growth of the offline (television broadcasting channel) and online (computer or mobile broadcasting channel), it is based on some analysis of its" the different kinds of entertainment broadcasting program audiences growth drivers either online broadcasting channel or offline broadcasting channel". This as informed by some published resesrch. For Forecasting aim, the TV audience market research also needs some input on the current relative profitability of the different entertainment broadcasting programs grouping. Some basic SWOT analysis, this was fairly raw and was used for further a series of key strategic questions that were worked through systematically over the three days. So, within three days, the entertainment program maker needs to make decision either it apply online broadcasting channel, from computer or mobile platform or offline broadcasting channel , from television only to let audience to watch to feel more comfortable and visable enjoyable feeling.

The analytical process (Demystifying Strategy), such as growth driver analysis, competitor profiling, which compares one's own competitive strength against some key competitors. A progess in the form of a key question for use in competitive analysis, such as online television program competitors, the general traditional television program needs to spend some time on day three to make a series of visits of the online television entertainment program broadcasting competitors.

Hence, it is the whole strategic thinking to the online and offline television entertainment broadcasting program decision makers in order to decide how to implement their different kinds of unique offline traditional entertainment television programs to increase attraction to let the traditional offline television entertainment program audiences won't be persuade to watch any online entertainment programs from online channel

more easily.
For example, in the TV series " Blackadder" a comedy set in historical times, there was a character known as Blackadder, renowned for getting in all kinds of scrapes. His companion, a scruffy and disgusting character called Baldrick, often used to help him try to get out of these scrapes, usually with disastrously funny results. A constant theme of this immortal series was that they would usually come back to the " cunning plan" to rescue them. When this was a humorous comedy invention , it inspired me in my long quest to demystify strategy.
Hence, any television entertainment broadcasting programs , such as this comedy entertainment program, the television entertainment broadcasting business needs to make decision either this comedy entertainment program is watched from online (computer or mobile electronic platform) or offline (traditional television) channels. How and why audiences are influenced to feel this comedy entertainment television program is more attractive to watch from online channel (computer or mobile platform)? If this comedy is watched from online channel , what the negative emotion, the audiences will feel? Hence, the comedy entertainment television program founder needs to gather data whether this comedy is either watched more attractive from online channel (computer or mobile electronic platform) or is watched more attractive from offline channel (traditional television). Thus, data gathering can help this comedy entertainment program founder can make more accurate online or offline television broadcasting decision either concentrating on watching from online watching channel or concentrating on watching from offline channel more to let its audiences to feel whether which online or offline channel can bring them to feel more entertainment enjoyable visual feeling.
Strategic thinking may include both kinds: One is operational thinking, it owns these characteristics, such as linear, deductive, pre-programmed , clear boundaries, safe. Another is strategic thinking, it owns these characteristics, such as iterative and unpredictable, inductive and intuitive, creative, ambiguous and fuzzy, anxiety provoking characteristics. So, any entertainment television program broadcasting designers or decision makers , they must need to learn how to apply strategic thinking method to design their any entertainment broadcasting programs to let audiences feel visual enjoyable feeling from either online or offline broadcasting channels. Finally, they also need to know these key criteia in order to achieve their any entertainment television broadcasting programs more attractive, they may

include: strategic attractiveness, financial attractiveness, implementation difficulty, uncertainty and risky and stakeholder acceptability. Moreover, any television entertainment broadcasting program decison makers need to evaluate strategic options to decide whether the television entetainment broadcasting program is chosen to watch from online or offline watching channel more.

● AI predicts online movie and television broadcast auidence watching entertainment choice behaviors

Artificial Intelligent technology can be one kind big data gathering tool to help

any businessmen to gather every day consumer shopping experiences and records from their transactions frequently from any shops, even it can help online television or movie broadcast companies to gather online movie or television watching entertainment enjoyers how their movies or television braodcast choices in order to predict whether what kinds of movies or television broadcasts are more popular to future online entertainment audiences market development. Then AI can gather these past consumer shopping behaviors data analysis to evaluate their past shopping experiences to make accurate prediction to future consumption behaviors for any kinds of merchants. I shall explain how and why AI can assist any merchants to predict future consumer behaviors how change.

For smart mobile exanple, it is one kind of communication devices, have become

constant computational companions that are increasingly being equipped with additional sensors. These accessories include accelerometers that are able to monitor our body movement, global positioning

system (GPS), chipests that measure our location, short-range radio protocols such as Bluetooth that can sense whom we are near, and even simple communication logs that are a measure of the evolution of our social network. A phone that is aware of a person's habits can make

inferences about schedules, suggest activities, or provide reminders without any manual prompting.

It can change its mode to accommodate various situations, for example, automatically turning off its ringer when in a movie threater and turning it back on after the filrm. A smart phone that knows more about people with interests similar to your gather or introduce you to a new restaurant just before you knew you wanted ro try a new place for dinner. So, smart phone is one good tool to record every consumer daily shopping activities or shopping habits or consumption behaviors in any shops easily. If the food merchant can gather all consumers' smart phone data to analysize whether he like to go to what food shops to choose to buy which kinds of food to eat for one month period.

Then, it can predict whether the consumer like what kinds of taste and it can predict the kinds of food and price level to general food consumers who can accept to consume, e.g.. it can apply smart phone tool to collect 200 food consumers' eating habit within one week. Then , it can follow these data to attempt to predict how their food consumption behaviors change in this food market.

Why does smart phone is one good tool to gather data to predict consumer behaviors. Because data from mobile phones can also provide insight into when and where consumers move from one locatoin to another, informatoin that can be critical when developing models of the spread od diseases , such as malaria and flu. In addition, reseachers are showing that changes in movement and conservation patterns captured by a phone with the appropriate sensors and software can indicate the oneset of illnesses. There are just a few early-stage examples of the potential of reality mining, the idea od using personal data to make peoples' lives easier and healthier, even consumer individual shopping habit and past shopping experience for any kinds of business reference. So, smart phone is a powerful way to extrapolate consumer behavioral information.

Hence, in the future, merchants can apply smart phone to record a growing number of consumers shopping behaviors daily. They have become facinated with their personal shopping data and combine all of the shopping information about themselves they can acquire, be it from mobile phone communication, computer activity, biometric sensors, video recordings or past shopping data recorded manually. This extreme sort of the different kinds of food or product choice cataloging and quantifying of different kinds of product or food data record is known as " lifelogging" . It has appealed to some merchants as a way to better understand all of their sample consumers' shopping habits.

- (AI) software that watches consumer habits in movie and television watching entertainment industy

The MIT reality -mining project provides a specific example of setting up a mobile phone-based study to collect personal data. For one research, a quick web search turns up a number of sites that sell software to be installed on Iphones, BlackBerrys, Android phones, and Windows
Mobile and Symbian operating system phones. The software is targeted at parents worried about their teen's phone actigity as well as at employers who want to monitor employees' use of company-supplied phones, and at people who want to catch spouses they suspect of cheating. It's important to note that differnt regions have different laws for collecting data from people's mobile phones legally, permission from the person who owns the phone or ownership of the device and/or contract is required. Thus, merchants must need to be permitted from the country's legal system and the smart phone users' permission in order to decide to apply smart phone to gather its sample customer individual shopping behaviors.

● Lifelogging can capture the flow of every online audience watching behavioral data

Clearly, there are myriad ways to collect data about the individual consumer every shopping behavior. It's also clear that there currently is no method for collect different types of data, which may be captured automatically by (AI) software, or produced and logged manually. But a growing subset of people are trying to create such a method for logging part or all of their lives: anything about the consumers themselves past per week shopping times and shopping kinds and consumption amount can be quantified.

Lifelogging as a trend is somewhat more popular i ncommunities of technically oriented people. Some of these people have created internet and mobile phone applicatons for logginf data, specialized hardware sucn as wearable cameras for capturing video and images, which can record any consumer behavior, for example, supermarket can install (AI) video cameras to capture every customer individual different kinds of food purchase in order to evaluate whether brand of food is the most popular, ad spreadsheet templates for recording a range of daily behaviors such as types of food consumed and emotions felt. Lifelogging fills in the gaps left by other data-collectoin methods and attempts to combine all the data in a cohesive framework that explains the individual quantitatively.

Ultimately, this types of work has a potential. One obvious applicatoin is that lifelogging allows people to see their habits amd how small changes in behaviors affect the rest of their lives, but these are more far-reaching possibilities as well. Today, some of the most lifelogging projects involve automatically capturing images and video.

In late 2009, Vicon a company that makes motion-capture systems, licensed technology developed that automatically takes a series of pictures through the day. Microsoft's Sense Cam hardware consists of a wideangle lens and a number of different electronic sensors, including light-intensity and light color sensor, a passive infrared (body heat)
detector, a temperature sensor, and a multiple -axis accelerometer. SenseCam can be programmed to take a picture at a regular interval or when changes in the wearer or environment, recorded by the seneors, trigger a photograph to be taken.

- How can apply smart phone to gather online audiences record and predict every future watching television programs choice change

Hence, future (AI) artificial intelligent technological product, e.g. smart phone can be the best tools to replace video cameras or computer tool or internet communication to gather consumer individual shopping behavioral data in order to make the most accurate past every daily consumption behavioral prediction. A clever example of using personal data to improve a person's health, still in the early stages, seeks to find which behaviors, locations, and social interactions are associated with smoking.

If the factors that contribute to someone lighting up are known, engineers can feasibly build a monile phone application, for instance, that recognizes a potential smoking situation. It might provide feedback, such as prompting the smoker to chew a piece of gum instead. It's also reasonable to assume that the methods developed in the smoking research project might be applied to other types of consumption behaivor, such as research why the consumer chooses to buy the kind of product to use frequently, or why the consumer only chooses to buy the brand of products to use frequently, why the consumer often choose to go to the shop for shopping etc. different types of consumption behavioral research. So, such as research online audience watching television broadcasting entertainment programs choice case, smart phone can be applied to gather their watching behaviors to predict what the factors influnce online audiences' watching changing mind any time more accurately

Instead of online television is popular to be accepted to any audience nowadays, I feel that any movie products ought follow music products to develop to digital media entertainment channel more than traditional television watching channel in order to attract many audiences. I indicate the reasons as below:

The cloud technological development is rapid, any music listeners or moive audiences can download any songs to listen from cloud channel easily. The cloud has been used as a metaphor to denote the internet since the latre 1960s and early 1970s, when Vinton Cerf, Robert Kahn, Robert Metcalfe, Leonard Kleinrock, Larry Roberts and many others invented the technologies behind the network of networks. A cloud was considered to be a useful and enough symbol

that could be used to summarize all the resources, cables and gadgets conneting the computers at the nodes of the network. These days, the cloud technology

is still used as a metaphor for the internet, but it also convenys other meanings. For more than 20 years, the computer company Sun Microsystems pushed the slogan " The network is the computer". Sun suggested back in those days that the resources in the Cloud would soon become so powerful that the computers at the network nodes would no longer have to be sophisticated and expensive bur could be made extremely simple and cheap. Eventually, technology dod not choose

exactly that path, bur in some respects, the cloud is the only field ofmusic to emphasize how the music industry has completeky shifted its centre from the physical to the virtual from the Disk to the cloud. Manyn years have passed since young party-goers relied on CDs for music, and today it is also less common to play MP3s stored on their computers or iPods. Instead, increaingly, they listen to music from YouTube, last or other Web-based music service; or they download a party mix from a file -sharing network such as LimeWire. Music is no longer something that mainstream audiences own and collect music is in the cloud.

So, movie industy ought follw music industry, I means that any kinds of movie can be download from cloud to watch. It can bring this advantage, for example,the movie manufacturer can evaluate how many audiences number, they choose to watch its movie among the other movie competitors every month, every week , even every day. So, it can gather the data to know whether their click times to watch its movie every day. Then it can compare their visitors' click to watch its movie times between other similar kinds of movie manufacturers whether whom have more click times to watch their movies every day. Consequently, it can analyze their click times data to attempt to find whether what factors cause it have less visitors number to click its movie to watch on the day. So, cloud technology can help movie manufactuers to gather data to predict how and why their audiences number can either increase or decrease as well as finding what the factors influence their watching tastes to the movie change suddenly.

Nowadays, movie and music industry is encountering new economy period. In the new digital media movie or music economy, it is still important to know how the audience uses intellectual property , but it is more or less impossible to regulate and police that use. I borrow a terms from network theory,connectivity to explain the new situation. Connectivity is a meausre of how well the members of a network are connected. A network is considered to have a high level of connectivity if most of its memebers are connected to each other.In a network with high connectivity, information , money, norms etc. easily flow between the members. Because cloud technology can let movie or music audience download any kinds of movie or music
to listen free charge usually as well as they can apply facebook to discuss their watching or listening feeling to the kind of movie or music immediately. So, cloud technology can bring good emotion feeling to have chance to let them to reflect their feeling after they watch the movie or listen the song from cloud technological download. Othewise, watching CD movie audiences or listening CD song listeners can not reflect their emotions to let their members to know immediately from facebook social media channel easily after they either go to cinema to watch the movie or buy the movie CD to watch from televison or go to the hall to listen the music or buy the music CD to listen from computer. So, cloud technology will change movie and music entertainment players'entertainment channel from cinema or music hall to online digital media channel. So, any movie manufacturers ought need to consider how to allocate their every movie time to let audiences to download to watch from cloud technology. Because every movie audience individual watching time has different long or short time watching need. So, they need to allocate different movie time to let them to watch from online channel.

Reference

Bigne, Enrique (2005). The impact of internet user shopping patterns and demographics on consumer mobile buying.

Falk, Louis, K. et. al (2005) " E-commerce and consumer's expectations: What makes a website work". Journal of website promotion, 1(1), 65-75.

Parasuraman, A., Zeithaml, V.A. and Berry L.L. (1988) SERVQUAL: A multiple-item scale for measuring consumer perceptions of service quality. Journal of retailing, 64, 12-40.

9 798885 558327

Printed by Libri Plureos GmbH in Hamburg,
Germany